Discovering Your Purpose

Be the YOU You're Meant to Be

Tammy Ogren, Ph.D.

Discovering Your Purpose

In this book, Dr. Tammy Ogren shares her personal journey to transform her life to align with her personal core values and to apply her natural strengths to walk a path that suits her natural abilities, personality, and core values. She provides examples, mistakes, and activities guiding you to identify your uniqueness and purpose.

In an interactive, practical manner you will receive tips, tools, and techniques to identify your personal strengths, energy drains, natural abilities, personality, core values and more.

If you are looking to identify your unique purpose, you will appreciate this story.

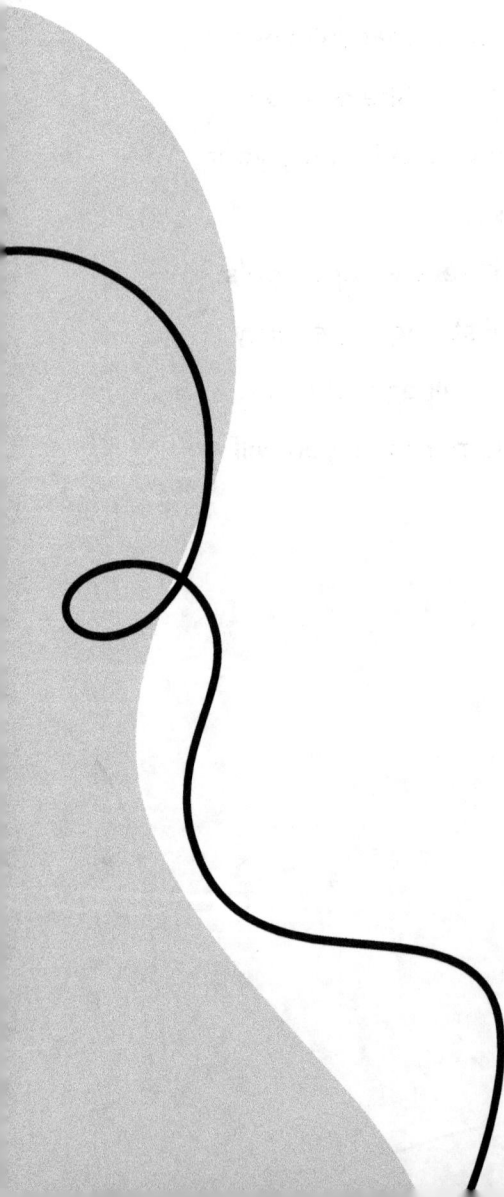

Table of Contents

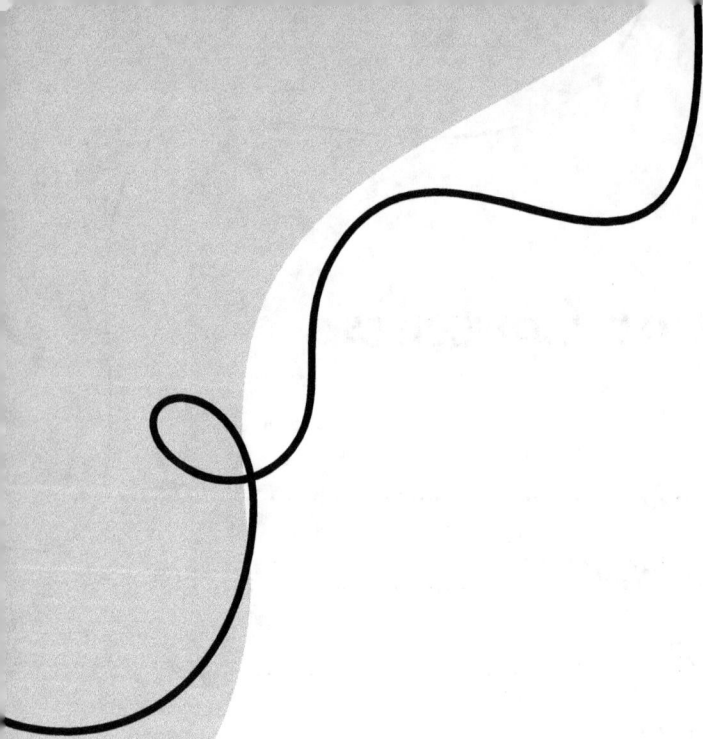

Foreword

Starting off with a personal mission to find her own personal purpose, how to integrate that into her life, in a way that made Dr. Ogren who she wanted to be, and as she says, "spending 90% of her time on the things she was intended to be doing and enjoyed doing as opposed to doing the things she despised doing or was mediocre at doing", caused Dr. Ogren to develop a process for herself. She then converted that process into a course that she taught to students at the collegiate level, both to adult learners that were returning to school and to young people. Through this course, she helped them to understand that their life's work could align to their natural attributes and gifts as well as those things they truly got joy from, which resulted in them living and working in areas where they were really energized. She taught that class, which was really an output of her own personal journey, for well over a decade and she got so much amazing feedback from students and graduates who would come back and tell her about it that she thought it was important to share it with more people beyond who she could just personally teach.

This book is the result of that feedback and desire to share beyond her personal reach. It has been written in a very brief way to get you a portion of the value that you might get by being able to participate in a course with her. But really, this journey is about you and taking the time to really reflect on the things where she suggests you spend time. And, if you'll do that, I have every confidence that you'll gain a lot of insight about yourself and an understanding of how what you want to do and what you should be doing, given the gifts that you've been given, considering the way we all uniquely operate in the world, can make your life so much more meaningful. And the fantastic thing about that is that where there are more people who are doing the things they are intended to do and the things they are gifted to do, I actually think that benefits us all in a way that I don't know if any of us really personally understand. I thank you for picking up this book and I really hope you enjoy the content. A few comments from Dr. Ogren's past students are on the following page.

"This was an excellent course and relevant to my day-to-day life. I have more tools in my toolbox and will share with others what I have learned. Thanks."

"Dr. Ogren was very personable and helped me to understand my potential. I had a lot of moments where I found myself glued to the topic that she was teaching."

"Thanks for this feedback. I am in a very interesting and transitional time in my life. Thank you for helping me be aware of my internal thoughts. With so much currently changing, and the pending changes that I know are coming, I am all over the place emotionally and intellectually. I am confident what I learned helped me in my work life."

"I must tell you how much I truly enjoyed your class. It opened my eyes to so many possibilities. I have been approached by a manager regarding an open position. It is something I would not have even considered before. I do not believe this offer would even be near me if it wasn't for your class.

"I love the fact that she talked about her personal experiences and used them as examples. She's a good speaker and a good teacher. She brought a lot of personal stories into the course to illustrate her points."

"This course was interesting, fun, and enlightening. It allowed me to look within myself and to understand others. I already had an idea of what I want to do in my retirement and this course will help me to go about that in a way that is beneficial to myself and to others. Now I know what motivates me. The course was well thought out and I cannot really think of any changes."

"As a retired teacher, I appreciated all the up-to-date teaching techniques that I learned through Tammy Ogren's lectures. That was not a stated purpose of the course, but just came through the story telling that she did throughout the course. There were many, many little nuggets of wisdom too of how to think about life and unexpected adventures into other things we might think about and study like Emotional Intelligence and Transitions. Very well-organized course, meticulously planned for students to learn in their own style and at their own pace. Very well adapted to changing times and supportive of all the participants. It became a very safe space for the students to express themselves and explore their purpose. Thank you."

"K. has left us now. Shortly after she took your course, she found out she had an aggressive form of cancer and passed away at the beginning of this year. She said through that journey, your course focused her on what was important in her life and what was important for her to do before she passed. She had arranged her own memorial and it was beautiful. She spent time with her family and friends and was ready for what she knew was her final day."

Introduction

My wish is that the process outlined in this book, along with my personal journey, my aha and uh-oh moments, provide you with a window into the possibilities that are trapped inside you! My hope is that you get to experience what I know exists…to find, know, and love *the you that you are meant to be.*

It took me many years to realize that I have uniqueness created and instilled in me intentionally and purposefully. I always believed that this was the reality; however, I used to believe it was someone else's reality and not really my own truth. For the voice in my head told me so, and sometimes the voices I surrounded myself with told me so, but guess what? I learned that I can control that truth. I can choose what I believe about myself, and I can change how I see myself in the mirror. The power of free will allows us to break free from that which binds us and stops us from fulfilling our own purpose.

So what is *purpose*? It is who you are when you dig deep and connect with your inner self—that truest part of your soul that only you know. It's your unique skills, personality, and talents. It's the unique way you think, make decisions, and process thoughts. It's those things that drive you toward certain behaviors, words, and decisions when you are your truest self...your best self...your easiest self...your most fulfilling self...your proudest self.

We each have a unique purpose. I believe that we're created intentionally and that our uniqueness suits us. It benefits us, and we are each capable of using our uniqueness in the world to impact others. *Our purpose is our meaning. Our purpose is our significance.*

The way I think and move through the world is right for me. And the way you think and move through the world is right for you. We are each able to do things uniquely different from others. I feel passion about things that you don't, and you feel passion about issues that I may not even think about. The way we feel ease is all part of what makes us uniquely "us" individually.

You have a unique voice and interact with the world in a way that is uniquely yours. You will connect with people I may never connect with because we see the same world in our own distinct fashions. You look at it differently than I look at it; we approach situations differently.

We are all on a fairly short journey on this earth, and we have a responsibility to ourselves, to our God, and to each other to be our best, to engage, and to apply our unique purpose where and when we should.

My intent in writing this book is that you identify and develop your own truth as I have identified and recognized mine. My real hope is that you understand your true self to discover your purpose. My greatest desire is that you get to experience the freedom, the rightness, and the ease that come in living and working within your uniqueness.

I spent many, many years prayerfully researching, seeking how to live in that space, because I believed it existed. I now live in that space during the majority of my life. My work is 90 percent within my unique purpose, and in my personal life, I continue to focus and refocus my relationships and my interactions toward my true self and unique purpose.

Because I believe you have the ability within you to do the same, I have created this unique method of transformation to provide a path for you to reach that potential. Go forward, and leave the world a better place than you found it.

Be the unique you that you are meant to be.

Watch for these:

AHA MOMENT

We all have those moments where time stands still and we know—we just know—what we are supposed to learn in that moment. I share aha moments from my life throughout this book. Share your aha moments on Facebook at ExpandWithPurpose or email me at togren@ ExpandWithPurpose.com

UH-OH!

When I make mistakes, I used to focus on regret, disdain, or shame. Now, I try to focus on learning something from the situation to be better tomorrow than I was yesterday.

LET'S DO IT! ACTIVITY

In these activities, I share my experience and offer you opportunities to explore the topic deeper through personal actions.

Remember Your "Why"

O ne More Thing Before We Start...

Before we can really live in our awesomeness, we must

be clear on what that awesomeness is!

So, as you work through this process, please, please, please do this for me.

First, be open to your own truth.

Second, set aside all physical, mental, or financial limiting beliefs that you or others have placed on you. We know that life today has real hurdles, but for this process to work, you have to set them aside; we'll come back to them. Limiting beliefs are those reasons you believe you can't...can't accomplish more, be something different, reach your dreams...on and on. We tell ourselves stories that relate to why we can't have, be, or do...Before we can even think about exploring our own purpose, our potential or our truth, we have to deal with these limiting beliefs. If we don't then we see them creep into our thoughts about our potential.

So let's start...Right now, take out paper, index cards, or Post-it notes. We are each different, but maybe start with a dozen papers. On each piece of paper, write down one limiting belief. What is holding you back from making a change toward living and working within your unique purpose? I had a lot, but I'll share a few of mine here:

Limiting Beliefs

I have responsibilities I can't ignore. I have to pay the mortgage and the bills.

My partner expects me to make as much money as I have been making.

What if I don't have uniqueness?

I want to be there for my children—how could I do something so intense for myself.

It's too late in my life to change my path now—I'm too old.

What if I figure out a higher purpose but can't find a way to make a living at it?

I'm afraid of being foolish.

Now really focus on those limitations for a moment. Read them out loud and let them sink into your soul. What emotions are you experiencing? Fear, embarrassment, doubt? Something else? Don't ignore it, don't look away. Face the emotions and feelings head-on and acknowledge your reality. Only when we face our reality can we change it, embrace it, or leave it. One by one, as you let the limitations sink into your soul and you acknowledge your emotional or physical responses, note the emotions you experience on your paper. Use a different color to write down your emotions.

Do you struggle with how to define emotions beyond the big 7: happy, sad, mad, bad, afraid, surprised, disgusted? Use this emotion wheel to look beyond the big categories. If you haven't done this before, it might take you some time to really identify the emotion aligned a specific limiting belief.

Emotion Wheel

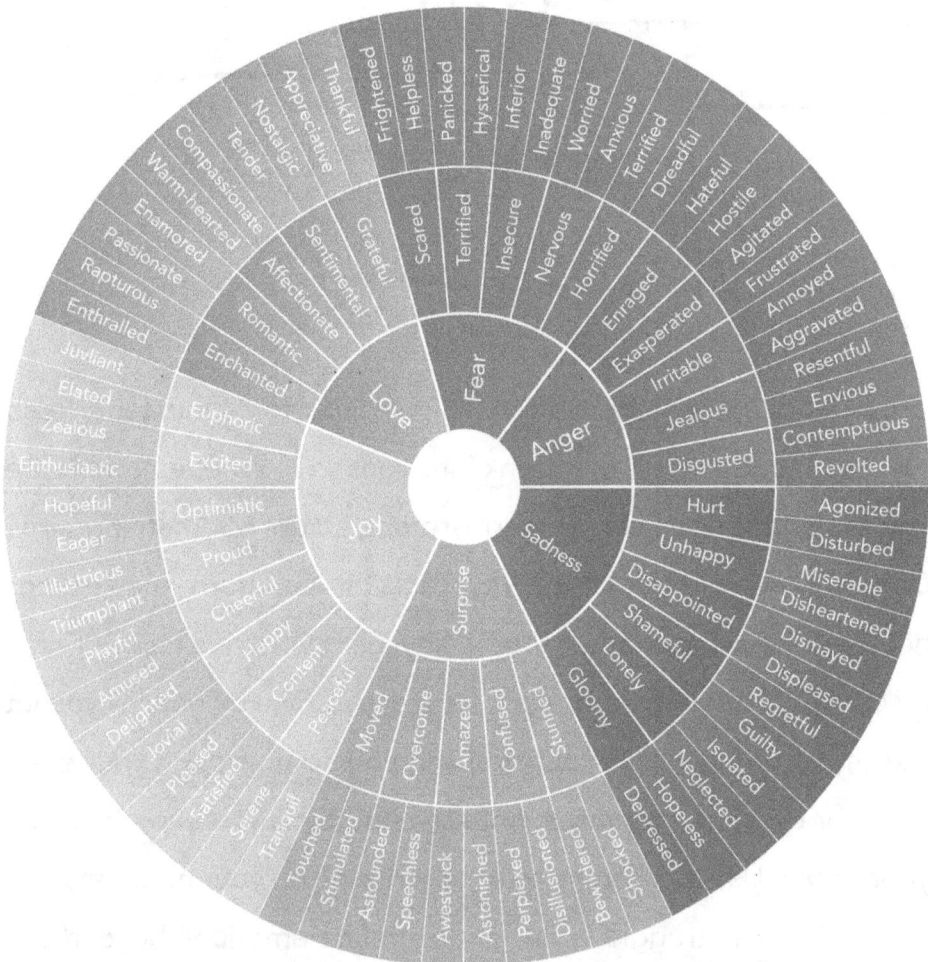

Originated by Dr. Plutchick

Some of my emotional and physical reactions follow:

Emotions Aligned to My Limiting Beliefs

My partner expects me to make as much money as I have been making.

ANGER. RESENTMENT.

What if I figure out a higher purpose but can't find a way to make a living at it?

EMBARRASSED. CONFUSED. HEART BETS FASTER.

I'm afraid of being foolish.

EMBARRASSED. SELF-DOUBT.

It's too late in my life to change my path now—I'm too old.

SADNESS. DEFEAT. DISAPPOINTMENT. HEAVINESS IN MY HEART.

I want to be there for my children—how could I do something so intense for myself.

SELFISH. SCARED.

Next, take out a clean piece of paper and write one of the limiting beliefs down. Next, consider the reasons that belief is not true. Is it what someone told you? Is it your real truth? No – it's a story that we tell ourselves, but there is a liberating truth for each limiting belief. Here are mine, as example:

Liberating Truths

Limiting Belief:

It's too late in my life to change my path now-I'm too old.

Liberating Truth:

At my age, I have much experience and knowledge to change with intention.

————

Limiting Belief:

I'm afraid of being foolish.

Liberating Truth:

I can look at myself and laugh. I know that I can learn from this experience.

————

Limiting Belief:

What if I find my higher purpose and can't make a living at it?

Liberating Truth:

Someone else is paying for the talents I possess. I am capable of finding them and learning how to be paid for my value.

Limiting Belief:

My partner expects me to make as much money as
I have been making.

Liberating Truth:

I am capable and smart and we can create a new budget, figure out
a new plan, and reevaluate our finances.

———

Limiting Belief:

I want to be there for my children-how could I do
something so intense for myself.

Liberating Truth:

I am capable of doing more than one thing and will always
put my childrens' needs first. That doesn't mean I can't do
something else.

Now, put these papers into a drawer, a box, an envelope, or somewhere you can't see them through this process. We know they exist, and they are real fears and limitations, but it's impossible to openly explore the truth of your inner self and your potential with those front and center.

Trust me, we'll come back to them. Just for now, set them aside and allow yourself the freedom to dream. Alright now, let's get started.

Remember Your "Why"

We find, know, and love our authentic selves by understanding our reason for being; that is our "why." We each have purpose, unique talents, skills, passions, and motivations that drive us to do what we do best, love what we do, and impact others in the doing. We so often take these attributes for granted because we are raised in cultures that teach us that to succeed, we must work hard.

Don't Make It Harder Than It Needs to Be

What if the reality is that we succeed when we do those things that are easiest for us, the things we are passionate about, and those things we innately know how to do? When we rest in the reality of our authenticity, life is calmer. Life is so full of challenges, often beyond our own control or understanding, but there is definitely a peaceful presence when I am in the space that fits my uniqueness. My personality is accepted and right for the situation, I'm driven through my internal motivators, my skills are applied with more ease than when I work in areas of frustration. When I get to work in the areas I am passionate about, I am so much happier and relaxed and just…well, just comfortable in my own skin. I guess it's easier—easier to just accomplish and do what's at hand. It's like rowing down the river…versus carrying the canoe through the low spots.

AHA MOMENT

We were canoeing with family friends when our sons were eight. As they floated down the river together, both in their first rowing experience, their canoe got turned around backward. Together, in sync, they stood up, turned around, sat down, and kept rowing. Watching them deal with this problem as nothing more than an insignificant nuisance brought us to tears in laughter. They didn't try to turn the canoe back around, against the current, as we would have. They didn't consider doing it "right" by keeping the helm at the front. They just adjusted and kept moving. No discussion, no argument, no pivoting for power. We can't always control the current, but we can adjust ourselves to the situation and keep going.

Embrace YOU.

You are not an accident—you are purposefully designed. Personality, skills, unique talents, passions, and motivations combine to make you...you. Know it and be OK with it. For years, my son has told me, "You do you, Mom." Be more than OK with it; accept YOU, look in the mirror and wholly accept the YOU that you see looking back at you.

Wait...what? Be OK with "you." accept you—um, but what about...*No!* I scream in my head. Love who you are. You are the you that you were meant to be. That is not an accident. Say it with me: "I am who I am, purposefully and intently." There is real value in looking at yourself in a mirror, smiling, and saying, "I love you." Have you really looked at yourself? Look long enough to get past your hairstyle or your features—to look at yourself deeply. Sometimes people struggle with the idea of saying, "I love you," so maybe you need to start with "I like you." I tried it, and yes, it's awkward and I only did it when no one was around, but...it also felt good. How can anyone else like me if *I* don't like me? I took it a step further and looked at what I *love* about myself.

✓ LET'S DO IT!
ACTIVITY

Stand in front of a mirror and really look at yourself. Look at the physical you and acknowledge what you like about yourself (and, oh yeah, only think about what you see that you appreciate!). Look beyond what you see. Consider your spirit, your personality. There is much to love about yourself.

Your turn:

I love _____

_____

I love _____

_____

I love _____

_____

2

Don't Play Small

What does it mean to "play small"? It is when you don't give your opinion for fear of rejection, or when you overcompensate for another's shortcomings, or when you hide your accomplishments or abilities to allow someone else to look stronger, smarter, or just better in their own or others' eyes. It's when you hide your light so as not to overshadow someone else's light. You make fun of your weaknesses instead of owning it and moving on. You say nothing when your strengths are questioned. You exaggerate a mistake or allow it to be joked about for years. It is when you downplay your success so as not to make another feel inferior.

We can find ourselves surrounded by 1 of 3 categories of people.

The Braggart

The person who did everything right, who knows more than you, who did it better than you, drove farther, made more, was more successful.

The Humble

To be humble is a virtue, but you can also be *too* humble. For every strength can be overdone and turn into a weakness. Are you too quick to preface the positive with what you did wrong, or to just dampen your successes? The humble can get overlooked in work and in life. They can be unseen.

The Confident

The person who has found the balance between humility and arrogance. The Confident describes the person who knows what he/she *is*, and accepts both their strengths and weaknesses.

We are only responsible for ourselves. I lived a lot of my life carrying the responsibility for others: for their well-being, their confidence, their success, their reputation, and even their position in our social and family circles. But, at the end of the day, we are solely responsible for our self as an individual: what we think of our self, how we value our self, the value we place on our self, what we say, what we do with our purpose, who we impact. We should only hold the tape measure of ourselves up against our own potential, not anyone else's.

I understand, in the depths of myself, what it means to define and measure success against others' expectations for me. I doubt I'm alone. When we truly breathe deep, understand who we are meant to be, accept our own truth, and drop away the façade we are living, leaving behind pretense or shame, only then are we free. Then we are free to be the authentic self we are meant to be.

AHA MOMENT

Playing a New Year's Eve card game where players submit a card they hope the dealer connects to, it was my turn as dealer. In the stack of cards handed to me by the other players, my attention focused on a card with the word "overcompensate." I can't remember the game, or the rules, or even what the goal was. But I remember that white card with the word staring at me and time stopped for a moment. It just stopped right there in the middle of a late-night celebratory social gathering. I was in another place. The friend who gave it to me said, "I've been holding that card all night waiting for your turn." In his honesty, I felt many emotions...none of them positive. It opened me up to the embarrassing fact that I'd been more focused on overcompensating for others' shortcomings than focusing on my own strength and power.

Ugh... That's what playing small means...

Be watchful for messages that speak your truth— you don't know how they might be delivered to you!

OVERCOMPENSATE

Embracing Our Own Vulnerability
Allows Others to Be Free

We need to embrace our own vulnerability as part of ourselves for others to grow. Yes, that's what I said: when we embrace our own vulnerability, we allow others to grow.

Vulnerability is the act of being authentic, even if that opens you up to criticism, to attack or to misunderstanding. Vulnerability is not weakness, but it is acknowledging our truth, and that may include recognizing the parts of us that are great and the parts of us that aren't.

Authenticity is knowing, owning, and loving the real you, and only when we embrace the whole of who we are can we be who we are meant to be. To know, love, and embrace ourselves, we must acknowledge those parts of our self that get in the way! We need to also know the part of us that is *not* our authentic self. I had a lifetime of behaviors and habits that I had to really dig deep with to think: Is this reaction a part of my true self, or is it a habit I developed in response to others' expectations? Don't let your ego or personal needs distract you. Don't let fear distract from your divine mission. Don't let your focus be on the wrong, the regret, the distraction, and don't panic! To feel safe, we must say yes to our self and in doing so, we may have to say no to someone else.

To be vulnerable means to recognize our truth – the good, the bad, and the ugly – and it allows others to be real. Being vulnerable is *not* shame, self-disrespect, or playing small. It is the authentic voice of our self, pulling back the curtain and showing what's real. Real in our own successes, our own power, our learning from failures.

Why do we see failure as dark and shameful? Why do we work so hard to hide in the darkest corner of our closet and protect our vulnerabilities from the world? Why do we stand in defense and verbose grandeur to cover up for those vulnerabilities? These responses are outward behaviors resulting from the underlying feeling of shame.

Shame is different things to different people. It connects directly back to our motivating values. Our values get rubbed like sandpaper on a smooth board that didn't need sanding. Instead of sliding like honey, the board gets roughed up and damaged. When, or if, you experience shame, dig deep to process the "why" of it. It may connect back to a formative event, a rooted belief, or one of your core values that motivates you from deep within (see Chapter 7). My ex-husband and I worked very hard to stay married for twenty-nine years, and when we decided to divorce, I felt real shame for a long time. Even in the knowledge that we were unable to be our authentic selves together, that I was stronger individually than with him, and that I couldn't really live in my uniqueness and stay, I went through a long process of overcoming the feeling of shame. We didn't do anything intentional to hurt each other; but we were not the same people as we were at 21 when we married.

We spend a lot of energy building the façade of our truth. We put on the face we choose for people to see, don't we?

Think of what we could have done with that same energy, brain power, and time spent keeping up the facade, had we opened the door to being real with others.

To be vulnerable, you have to balance the scales in your own mind. First, love your strengths, positive traits, personality, who you are to others, and the service you provide to this world.

Then, know your weaknesses. We will talk more about these in Chapter 8.

! UH-OH!

When I processed why I felt shame for my divorce, I realized it connected right back to one of my motivating values: achievement. For me, letting go of this marriage was a failure after hanging on so long. It was realizing that at the end of the day, I couldn't be what he wanted me to be. I couldn't be what he needed me to be. And he couldn't be what I needed. At the end of the day, we choose to be our own selves. Reframing the situation within that value, I slowly realized that I was now able to achieve living within the space of my own authenticity.

Pull your vulnerabilities out of the dark corner of the closet, write them down, look yourself in the mirror, and say them out loud. Embrace them for what they are—they just *are*—and embrace them without judgment. Don't place value on them. We put value on our weaknesses and our embarrassments; we have built stories around them, and we magnify them. Value comes in many forms:

Our time.

Oh my, what time I wasted doing xxx, thinking what I could do have done with that time if I spent it on my strengths.

Our confidence.

I knew I couldn't xxxx, Mom said I could never xxx. My sister was always better at xxx.

Our relationships.

My husband/wife/boss always said I was too xxx, that I didn't xxxx. I told people I would xxxx, and I didn't get it done.

Instead of recognizing these interactions as simply experiences that occur during our lifetime, we sometimes create facts and beliefs that we embed in our reality. I can easily move into believing I'm 'less than' because I've been told it so many times. I don't recognize it for someone else's opinion – that doesn't have to be my truth. Sometimes it just "is what it is." If we were all perfect, or even above average, in all things, we would be like a god, right? We would also be the most annoying friend! What a lonely place that would be! You can't be in your purpose if you don't know where your vulnerabilities are; it's actually a significant part of what your purpose is.

One way to uncover core vulnerabilities is to think about something that makes you feel embarrassment, failure, fear, or shame. Then ask yourself, "Why do I feel this?" You might have to ask yourself up to five times, digging deeper with each round, until you experience an aha moment. I think it's sometimes easiest to recognize our core values when we consider our triggers—those occurrences that cause these deep emotions.

We can actually find Confidence in identifying where we are Vulnerable. Let's try this...

Embracing Vulnerabilites and Finding Confidence

First – write down what you feel vulnerable about –
Ask yourself "Why" 5 times to go deeper and deeper into the
reason behind this vulnerability.
When you recognize the real reason – consider how to build that
into a confidence with a foundation that is strong.

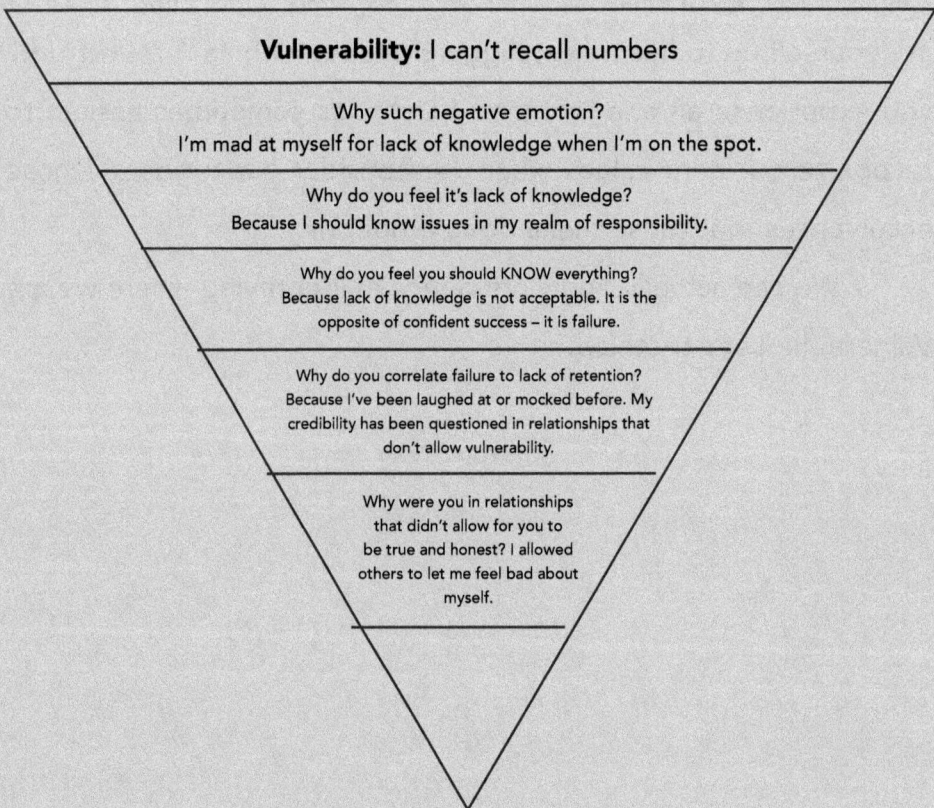

Vulnerability: I can't recall numbers

Why such negative emotion?
I'm mad at myself for lack of knowledge when I'm on the spot.

Why do you feel it's lack of knowledge?
Because I should know issues in my realm of responsibility.

Why do you feel you should KNOW everything?
Because lack of knowledge is not acceptable. It is the
opposite of confident success – it is failure.

Why do you correlate failure to lack of retention?
Because I've been laughed at or mocked before. My
credibility has been questioned in relationships that
don't allow vulnerability.

Why were you in relationships
that didn't allow for you to
be true and honest? I allowed
others to let me feel bad about
myself.

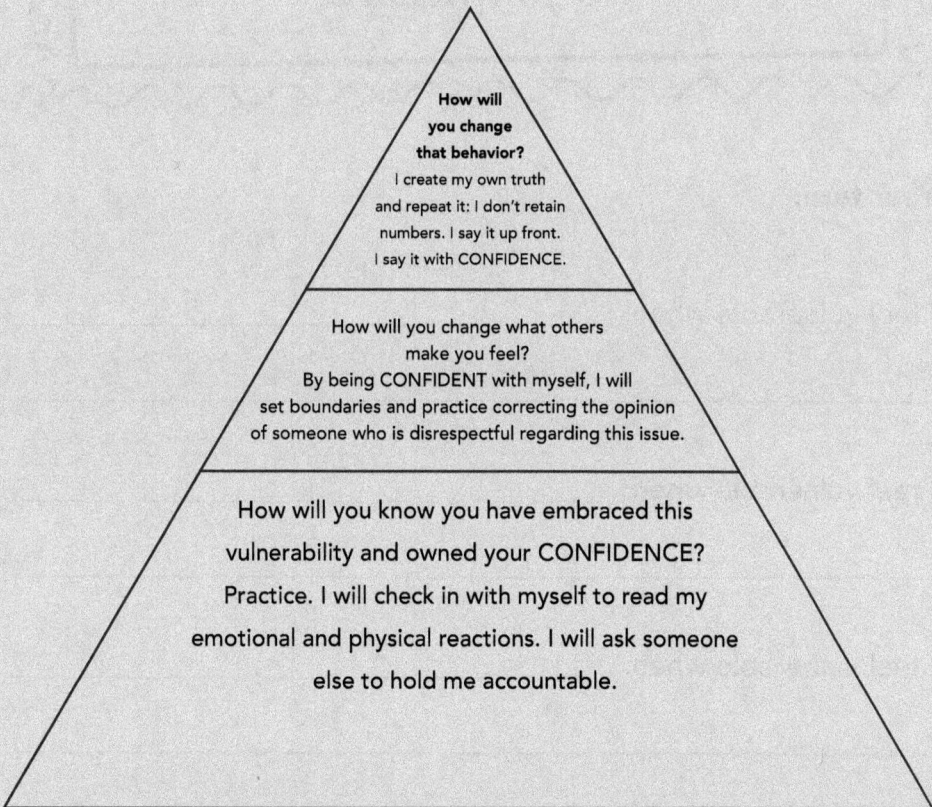

**How will
you change
that behavior?**
I create my own truth
and repeat it: I don't retain
numbers. I say it up front.
I say it with CONFIDENCE.

How will you change what others
make you feel?
By being CONFIDENT with myself, I will
set boundaries and practice correcting the opinion
of someone who is disrespectful regarding this issue.

How will you know you have embraced this
vulnerability and owned your CONFIDENCE?
Practice. I will check in with myself to read my
emotional and physical reactions. I will ask someone
else to hold me accountable.

☑ LET'S DO IT!
ACTIVITY

What vulnerabilities are you aware of now?
Look at yourself and acknowledge what you like about yourself (and, oh yeah, only think about what you see that you appreciate!).

Your turn:

I feel vulnerable when: _____

_____

I feel vulnerable when: _____

_____

I feel vulnerable when: _____

_____

Choose something you've listed above for this exercise of turning a VULNERABLE issue into a CONFIDENT stance.

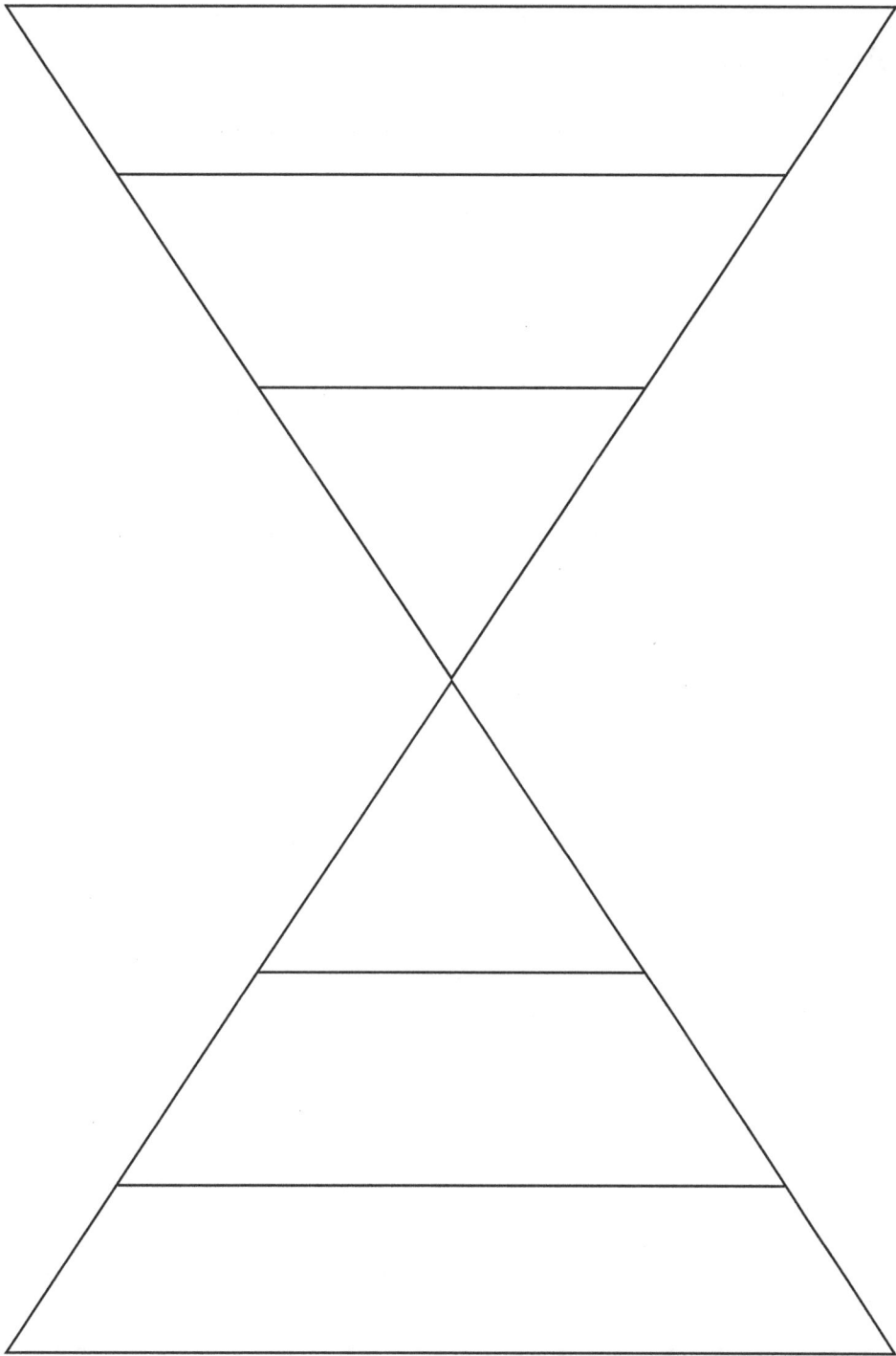

Notes

Chapter 3

Relationships Matter

T he journey of our past, our present, and our future makes up our lifetime and consists of the connections we travel through in this short time on earth. Think about all the people who have come and gone along the way. Aren't those the essence of our existence? In each interaction, there is an exchange of energy that impacts us. Consider the last interaction you had before reading this. On the surface, was it positive, negative, or neutral?

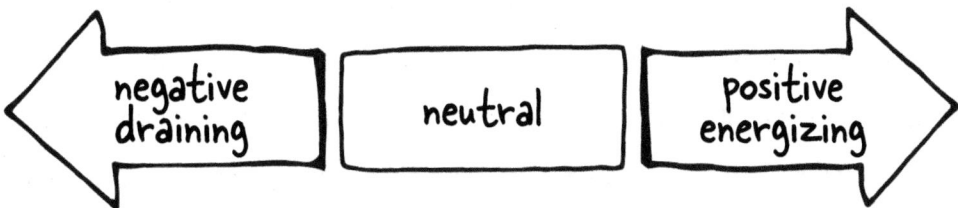

| negative draining | neutral | positive energizing |

All you really know about that interaction are two things: the energetic connection you felt and your perception of the interaction for the other person. Consider this: you don't know what the other person took away from the exchange; you don't know what they may recall later, you don't know what impact your interaction made on them or people in their realm of interactions. You don't know what impact that connection will have on a future interaction they have, whether it's now or years from now. You may not even realize the impact the interaction will have on you in the future... Your mind will actually pull experiences, no matter how seemingly small, from your mental archives to connect the experience to meaning in another time. Connections are constantly made in our lives.

Isn't our life really only about one relationship after another? At the grocery store, we interact with the cashier or we ignore them. We build relationships through an exchange of energy—that's the value we exchange to build on our commonalities. We may have a relationship that exists in a blink of an eye: a smile, an eyeroll, a handshake, a "thank you." We don't know the other side of the relationship; we apply our own thoughts about the moment onto others when we really don't know where the other person is

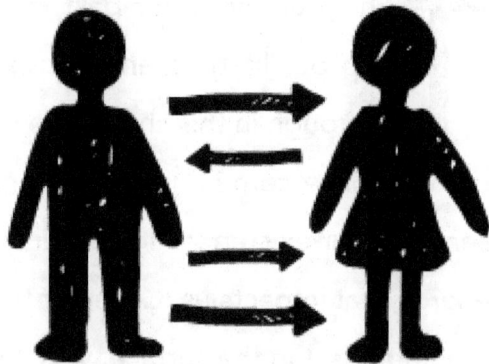

in that moment. In that moment of exchange, their reality may not be the same as yours!

What if every interaction you have with another person were not just an accident? We move through life collecting elements of others' essence that enhance, validate, or diminish our lives. What better goal than to be a person who enhances and validates others. With that goal forefront, would you do anything differently?

The most basic foundation of our life journey is our relationships and connections. Sometimes we build intentional, deep, and long-lasting relationships, but we also experience quick, connected heartbeats in moments of time with people in ways we may never know. If we are present in the moment, we can pick up emotional and physical cues by the look on their faces, the tone of their voices, or the reflection of their expressions. It can happen while simply standing in the grocery store line, walking down the aisle of a store, or pumping gas next to someone. Most days we connect with people. Think about the number of people you cross paths with in a normal day. What if, in each of those connections, we were making an impact? We unconsciously make many impacts every day. We can get so consumed with our own issues, our own world, and our own daily grind that we can easily influence others without realizing it.

Be mindful to look outside yourself and realize that you don't know what's going on with the people around you.

Do we choose our relationships, or do they choose us? Do

you place value on others by looking at them, by making swift judgments of trust based on sight? Or do you give others a chance? Do we miss out on the value of interactions and relationships before we even get to know the other person in our path? There are no levels in life; we all come from the womb the same and we end up in the ground the same. It's the space in between and what we do with it that makes the difference. Connecting with people is fundamental to everything. Why else are we here but to impact relationships and people along the way?

Positivity, acceptance, love, embracing each other, leaving people better than they were before we interacted. Is there really anything more important than that?

To be vulnerable, we must let go of the expectations from our self and others. To feel creativity in our soul, we must be open to vulnerability and newness. To authentically connect with others, we must open ourselves and drop our shield of self-protection to take the risk of connection. In toxic or abusive relationships, we must recognize that to be our authentic self, we must let them go for our true self to grow. When we are in relationships with someone who shames us to make themselves bigger or to one-up us, we must let them go to grow. We must be guided to healthy relationships that are real, honest, and deep instead of shallow and fake.

AHA MOMENT

I remember having a relationship with someone who exuded an oppressive energy. Looking back, I realize I spent years trying to overcompensate for it and bring them out of their "funk." Then I started tiptoeing around them to try to live around it without absorbing it. Neither were good for my own soul!

I was given this tip that changed me so much! When I followed it, it made me (1) smile and (2) feel like I controlled the situation instead of tiptoeing around it or owning someone else's problem!

I imagine myself spinning a bright pink, bulletproof glass bubble around myself. Only I can see it, but any negative energy bounces off it and it only allows positive interactions through...I choose what I let "in."

Wow—somehow the mind game or the experience helped me to be authentic and allow others' negativity to bounce off me.

I do it whenever I need to protect my own energy.

✓ LET'S DO IT!
ACTIVITY

Learn to protect yourself from negative and oppressive energy by:

1 Recognizing it for what it is.

Are you sending the energy out, or are you absorbing someone else's energy? STOP. Process. Where is the dark energy coming from?

Sit quietly and bring to mind someone who you've experienced negative energy or negative interactions with. Is it coming from you or them...or both? Allow the truth of the source of the energy to rise.

2 Release the negative.

Reject the negative while pulling your own positive energy up as a larger force so there is no room left for the negativity of others.

Close your eyes and focus on the negative energy. Draw it in and blow it out. Imagine it moving into the clouds, whisked away by the winds.

3 Use your creativity to protect yourself!

Shield yourself from allowing the negative back into your "space."

Consciously think of a mantra, a prayer, or an action of your own (feel free to borrow my pink bubble!). Practice so it becomes a natural reaction when you feel that negativity approaching in the future.

4 Change the narrative in your mind.

As the fearful, negative thoughts enter your mind, be your own alter ego and command that voice to "Stop talking."

Sit quietly, allowing your mind to wander. Breath slowly and with each indrawn breath, practice stopping the thought midsentence.

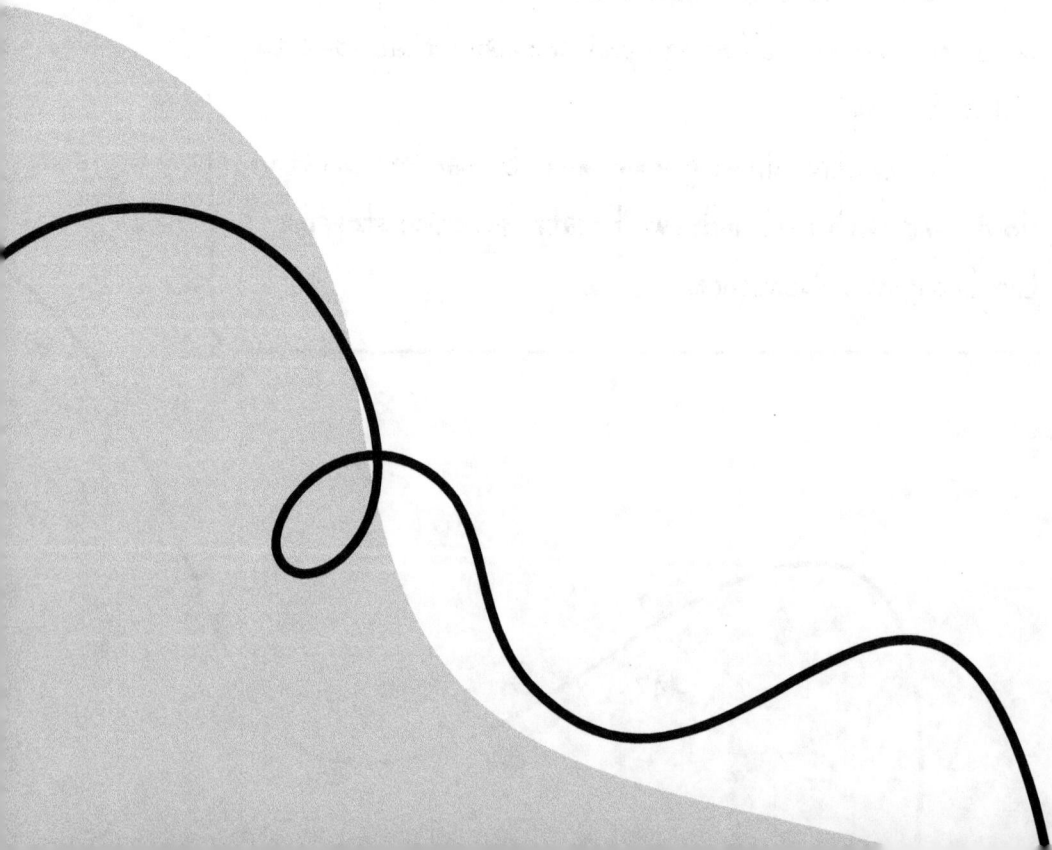

Forgiving Yourself & Others

Forgiveness is powerful. Holding grudges, resentment, and blame really only hurt you. The other person may not even know you feel the way you feel; they may not even realize when the relationship shifts or changes, but we too often hang onto this white-knuckled focused intent to not let the other person "off the hook." Yet, what good does that serve us? Holding onto the old pain can consume us; it creates an ongoing thought process that we can't get out of. It affects the energy with which we live; it can become the filter through which we see the world, and it can be so consuming that we may be the only one hurting.

As a young adult, I learned the hard lesson that forgiveness is about me—it's not about the other person. Forgiveness is about freeing myself from the emotional, physical, and mental pain and connection to the other person. Forgiving the other person isn't about letting them off the hook; it's not about saying that they are OK, or that I approve of what they did. It's really only about bringing my own soul to move on. It was the mental act of letting go of this intangible thing I was holding onto so tightly that it kept me connected to that person in my mind and my soul.

Forgiveness is not about forgetting; forgiveness is about releasing our negative emotions and thoughts, consciously letting them go and moving forward freely.

The first time my father left, I was one and a half years old and my mother was giving birth to my sister. He never really "came back"; he flitted in and out of our lives at his whim, and I replied by withholding myself from him. My sister responded in an opposite manner; she kept climbing out on the tree limb for him to cut it out from under her. I, on the other hand, quit climbing the tree. I spent so much time in my life waiting for my father to see the error of his ways, to apologize, but I realized that it wasn't in him. But, my withholding forgiveness was only hurting me—he didn't even really know how I felt. When I made the conscious choice to let go of the hurt and really forgive him, I experienced release and a weight lifted. Forgiveness is about releasing our weight, not the other person's.

Do you need to wipe the slate clean with anyone? Are you harboring resentment, grudges, unforgiveness? All this does is stop you from being your best; instead, clear the space for positive relationships, opportunities, and clarity. I really believe that, at its simplest, forgiveness is about acknowledging my hurt—looking at it for what it is, releasing it, and consciously letting go of the disappointment, the pain, or the expectation that the other person will admit wrongdoing or see the error of their ways. Because forgiveness is about me, it's internal, and the freedom comes when I let the negativity go. It's not easy, but it's powerful.

The trick is to control my thought process after actually forgiving and letting go. You may find your own trick, but as a fire lover, this works for me.

[warning—do this outside and carefully]

On several small pieces of paper, I write my issues down as fast as I can, listing whatever I'm feeling I need to release. I take a tin can and matches outside (a soup can works, as it's usually handy). Crumple the papers into little balls, or tear them into little pieces and place them in the can. Light them on fire.

As I watch the edges of the papers curl, turning into ash, I see the smoke floating up from the written words, past the can, into the universe, turning into air that I can't retrieve. I then say something like, "I release the xxx, I forgive xxx, into the universe so I have space for positivity in my future."

As the edges of the paper start to turn black and it curls up and smoke floats away, it is a mental sign for me that I have just committed that feeling, or emotion, or memory to the idea of letting it go into the air that carries it into the abyss of our universe. I can't grab that smoke back; it's not tangible, and as it goes into the air, it dissipates. Then as days go by and my personal thoughts turn back to wanting to resent or remember or replay, it's a conscious exercise to say to myself, "You already let that go and it's gone. STOP!" Replacing the soundtrack of my mind with a positive narrative is key.

Now it's your turn. Who might you need to forgive in order to move forward? Are you harboring anger, resentment, or disappointment about someone in particular? Might you need to forgive yourself? Maybe you need to let something go to make space for a new and promising future.

Moving forward is letting go.
Letting go is moving forward.

✓ LET'S DO IT!
ACTIVITY

Now it's your turn:

1 On a piece of paper, write the name of the person and the things you are letting go. Be specific. Write as much as you need to. Look at it, read it, think about it. Are you ready to let it go?

2 Write these words: "I forgive (name) for the acts/words/etc. of xxx and I let go of my (resentment, fear, disappointment, anger, etc.). I choose to move forward and to release the emotional hold he/she has on me through the act of remembering and hanging onto this injustice I harbor. I choose to let it go in order to fill that space within me with positivity and growth in anticipation for the future instead of harboring the past.

3 When you are ready, destroy it. Shred the paper and throw it away outside in a trash can or burn it outside (I use an empty soup can and a match outside to release it into the universe). Once it's gone, breathe deeply in through your nose and out through your mouth. I like to picture the release of the ugliness out of myself into the air.

4 In the future, if your mind draws it back in, stop it before it takes root. When that person comes to mind, breathe in the truth of your feelings. Breathe out the release.

Chapter 5

Finding the YOU that You ARE

Your "why" is the reason you exist. Why are you here? What are you meant to be? You're made uniquely you—with intentionality—with personality, with passions, with skills and strengths, with motivations—that make up this unique being that you see in the mirror. I think we often focus on what we need to change or fix. What if we spent as much energy building on our foundations and our strengths?

Understanding your personality explains what energizes you, how you take in information, how you make decisions, and how you interact with the world around you.

You have motivations different from other people. Those core values drive your behavior. It's the *why* you do what you do. They are internal passions that are triggered when they are touched, and they are triggered with strong emotions when they are disrespected. These things that motivate us drive us. They are our core values.

You have unique strengths and talents that you do without thinking; you have unique skills that you may not even recognize as special. We are brought up in a culture where we are told that we succeed through hard work and effort. What if we spent our time in those areas of strength, and only did the things that were easy for us? Peace, ease, and lower stress occurs when we are within our natural strengths. It doesn't feel like work.

What are you passionate about? What books are on your bookshelf? What do you google? What articles do you read? What podcasts do you subscribe to? What do you research "just be-cause" you are interested?

In the next four chapters, we will discuss each of these ele-ments in depth.

Embracing Your Personality

When we understand our personality, we better understand our real self. We can understand how we are innately wired, for each of us interact with and respond to the world in unique ways.

What is personality? Our personality simply describes how we interact in the world. I can't have a conversation about Purpose without talking about the impact of our personality on our life. I believe that we are born into the world with innate ways we think and interact with others. I think it's important to also recognize how formative events impact our lives. Impactful events, family situations, influential persons and more can leave impressions that stay with us into adulthood. Personality describes how we think, how we make decisions, how we are energized, and how we move through the world. We know, though, that those formative events, family values, parental expectations, etc. also play a significant role in how we interact in the world. While those are essential to recognize, we will focus here on the understanding of our personality to better understand ourselves and others.

Are you energized when you are interacting with large groups of people? Do you crave alone time to embrace your quiet thoughts and ideas? Are you a logical and rational thinker...a rule follower? Do you consider justice for all or the rights of one? Are you driven by empathy? Are you systematic, methodical, and organized? Do you religiously use to-do lists, checklists, and is your calendar color-coded? Does checking something of your list give you pleasure? Or are you generally looking for possibilities and opportunities? Do you love the abstract so you can interpret in your own manner? Or do you like the concrete, the realistic?

When I studied personality theories, I learned a lot about myself and others. Understanding your own and others' personality traits allows you to understand your natural tendencies to react in given situations, recognize environments where you are your best, and to realize why other situations create angst or stress.

There are many personality theories and assessments – just google personality assessment and you will see many. I'm an assessment nerd, so I take them all but my favored is The Myers Briggs Behavior Indicator (MBTI)® so that is my focus here, but there are many valuable personality assessments available.

The MBTI personality assessment is based on research by Carl Jung, a Swiss psychologist, who believed that individual preferences are innate or, as he labeled them, "inborn predispositions." He also recognized that these innate preferences interact with and are shaped by environmental influences including family, country, and education. He believed that our inborn predispositions do not change over time and that these are our natural preferences. However, how we use our in-born tendencies and out of preference choices are impacted by our environment, situations, other people, and our own expectations.

In the following chart, you will see an overview of the four areas of personality discussed in the following pages. Consider these areas each as having a continuum...you may fall somewhere between the polar opposites. We should avoid an all or nothing approach to labeling ourselves or others. We should avoid putting ourselves in a box. We are far too complex to think we only interact in one way.

Overview of MBTI Elements

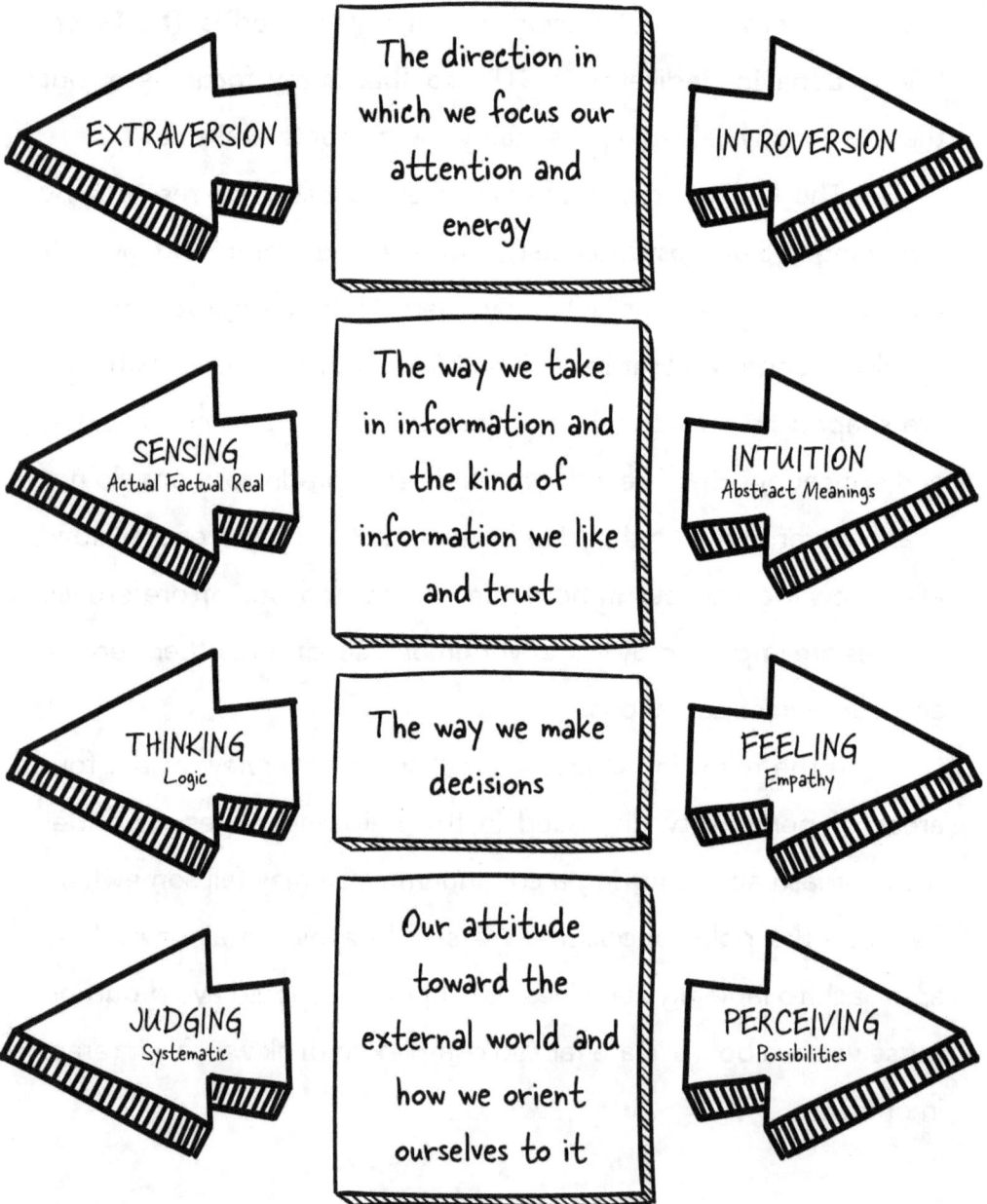

EXTRAVERSION

The direction in which we focus our attention and energy

INTROVERSION

SENSING
Actual Factual Real

The way we take in information and the kind of information we like and trust

INTUITION
Abstract Meanings

THINKING
Logic

The way we make decisions

FEELING
Empathy

JUDGING
Systematic

Our attitude toward the external world and how we orient ourselves to it

PERCEIVING
Possibilities

Extraversion and Introversion Explained: Where We Get Our Energy

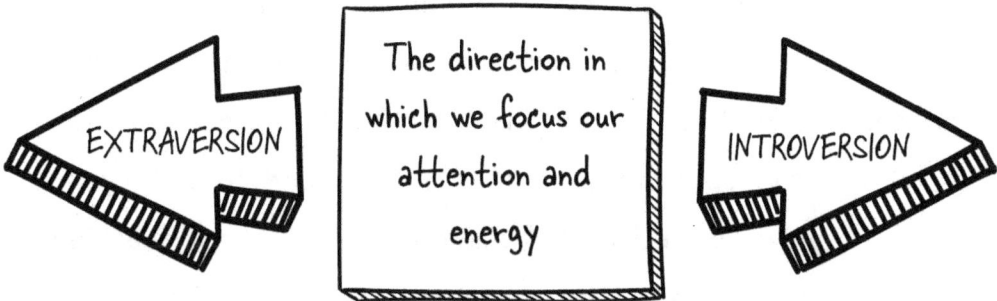

The direction in which we focus our attention and energy

EXTRAVERSION

INTROVERSION

People who prefer **Extraversion** focus their energy and attention outward. And they experience increase in energy from this outward experience. They are interested in the world of people and things. They prefer to communicate by talking with others, and they process their thoughts verbally. They may even say, "I didn't know what I was thinking until I said it out loud." They learn best by doing and discussing; they tend to be social and expressive, readily taking initiative in relationships.

People who prefer **Introversion** focus their energy and attention inward and are interested in the inner world of thoughts and reflections. They tend to prefer to communicate in writing and work out ideas by reflecting on them. They focus in depth on issues of interest and may be private and contained. They take initiative when situations or issues are very important to them.

Remember, we all use both preferences, but usually we do not use them with equal comfort. One might bring us joy while the other is just done 'as-needed'.

So lets think about this for a moment. I'm an introvert and when I realized my inborn need for time and space to think, create, and re-energize, I realized that I'm at my best when I provide myself with that space for internalizing. I've spent most of my career in very extroverted work – leading, consulting, and teaching in busy environments where I'm called on for interactions, much talking, quick decisions, and high external energy.

Before I understood myself well, without realizing it, I had habits that worked against me. For example, my calendar was packed with meetings and I would even be on my phone until I pulled into my driveway at the end of the day. From that point, the evening was often filled with busy conversations, nightly family dinners, kids, family, activities, and more...until we repeated it the next day. I remember a feeling of being worn out – even though I loved all the things I was doing.

After studying personalities, and mine in particular, I understood the impact of being an introvert in an extraverted world. I made some small changes that made large impacts. I gave myself a few minutes of alone time to just be quiet for moments. That re-energized me significantly. I learned that I could walk or sit in the sunshine for just a few minutes and – wow – I could absorb that quiet to re-energize quickly. I also started blocking time on my calendar for me – to think, to focus, to create, etc. In the early days I felt guilty about that. Now, I know that I'm at my best when I carve out space for quiet alone time.

That can sound so draining for some people who need interaction with other people to keep their energy. As an extrovert, you might find that too much quiet alone time is as draining as being active is for an introvert. To protect yourself, you may need to be sure you have people and activities to interact with or activities to participate in. In these days of virtual work, it is especially important for extroverts to recognize their energy sources and drains --- find what works for you to keep your energy rejuvenated!

We are all different! Protect your own energy and respect the needs of those around you!

Sensing and Intuition Explained: How We Take In Information

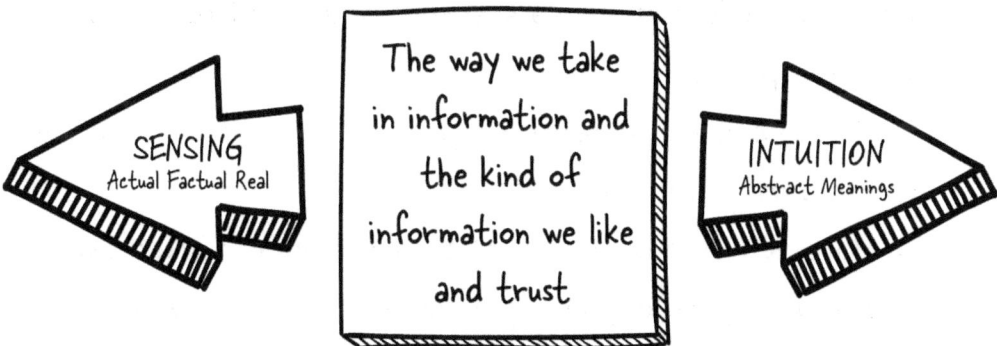

SENSING
Actual Factual Real

The way we take in information and the kind of information we like and trust

INTUITION
Abstract Meanings

People who prefer **Sensing** learn and take in information through their five senses of sight, sound, smell, touch, and taste. They tend to consider information in the realm of the actual, factual, and real. These are the folks who remember specifics and can store details of the past with acute observation. They build carefully and thoughtfully toward conclusions and prefer practical applications over ideas and theories. They take in and present information in a sequential, step-by-step fashion. They trust experience more than the unknown. They tend to believe what they know and experience – they trust it for what it is without any additional meaning.

People who prefer **Intuition** go beyond what is real or concrete and focus on meaning, interpretations, associations, and relationships. They are oriented to future possibilities more than actual, concrete, and past experiences. They tend to be imaginative, verbally creative, and see patterns and meanings. They remember stories and relate them to patterns. These folks may move quickly to conclusions and be comfortable following hunches. They take in and present information in a snapshot or a big-picture manner. They trust inspiration.

Remember, we all use both preferences, but we typically prefer and trust one more.

Have you ever been part of a conversation, walked away, and realized that two of you heard and interpreted very different versions of the conversation? How does that happen? Are one of

you lying? Was one just not paying attention? Not necessarily –
for this example, we will assume that both of you may really have
listened and absorbed the information. However, you did that in
separate ways. One may hear exactly what was said while the other
interpreted based on personal meaning.

It is so important for us to communicate with clarity to avoid
misunderstanding.

This also shows up when we teach someone something. We
tend to teach in the way we learn, but we need to understand that
we are more impactful to teach others in the way they learn. I've
learned to incorporate both aspects in my teaching and in important conversation – start with the big picture, followed by the details. This is an example of applying the concept to connect with all
types of learners.

The chart on the following page shows commonly asked
questions by the two types.

Common Questions by Type

SENSING	INTUITION
Concrete: What do we know? How do we know it?	Abstract: What could this mean?
Realistic: What are the real costs?	Imaginative: What else can we come up with?
Practical: Will it work?	Conceptual: Are there other interesting ideas?
Experiential: Can you show me how it works?	Theoretical: How is it all interconnected?
Traditional: Does anything really need changing?	Original: What's a different way to do this?

Thinking and Feeling Explained: How We Make Decisions

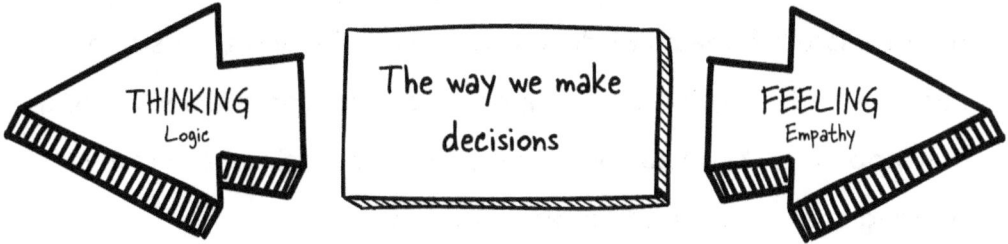

People who prefer **Thinking** instinctively make their decisions based on impersonal, objective logic. These folks are analytical and solve problems with logic. They consider cause-and-effect reasoning and strive for an objective standard of truth. They may be considered reasonable and tough minded. They think about fairness in terms of wanting everyone treated equally.

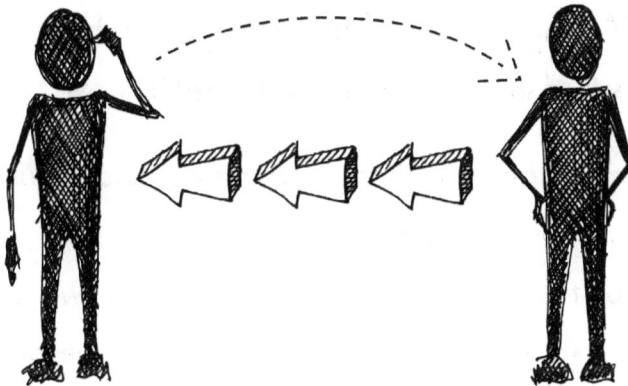

Making decisions by stepping back from the situation, taking an objective view

People who prefer **Feeling** instinctively make their decisions with a person-centered, values-based process. These folks are empathetic and make decisions guided by their personal beliefs. They tend to assess impacts of decisions on people, and they strive for harmony and positive interactions. They are compassionate and may appear tender hearted. They think about fairness in terms of wanting everyone treated as an individual.

Making decisions by stepping into the situation, taking an empathetic view

Remember, both processes are rational and we use both often, but usually not equally easily.

We aren't just one or the other 'type'; but we may have a first instinct to make decisions with one of these aspects as our instinctive mode. I believe it is so important to use both aspects, especially in major decisions. If you see yourself using one aspect more than the other, than recognize the importance of having someone different than you to bounce ideas and consider impacts of your decisions. The chart below shows examples of how different people think:

Common Questions by Type

THINKING	FEELING
Logical: What are the pros and cons?	Empathetic: What's really important?
Reasonable: What are the logical consequences?	Compassionate: What impact will this have on people?
Questioning: But what about...?	Accommodating: How can we get more people to agree?
Critical: What's wrong with this?	Accepting: What's right with this?
Tough: Why aren't we following through now?	Tender: What about the people that will be hurt?

A popular decision-making model, the Z-Model, uses these aspects to help people consider all the aspects of important decisions.

Z-Model for Decision Making

SENSING	INTUITION
Concrete	Abstract
Realistic	Imaginative
Practical	Conceptual
Experiential	Theoretical
Traditional	Original

THINKING	FEELING
Logical	Empathetic
Reasonable	Compassionate
Questioning	Accommodating
Critical	Accepting
Tough	Tender

Judging and Perceiving Explained: How We Interact in the World

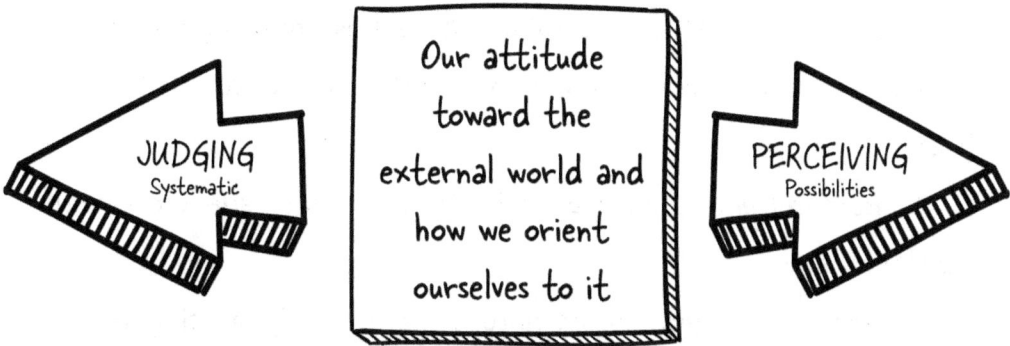

JUDGING
Systematic

Our attitude
toward the
external world and
how we orient
ourselves to it

PERCEIVING
Possibilities

People who prefer **Judging** want the external world around them to be organized and orderly. They look at the world and see decisions that need to be made. They tend to be scheduled, systematic, methodical, and naturally organize their lives. They value closure—they have to-do lists, up to date calendars, orderly cabinets, and their work is completed systematically and methodically. These folks may enjoy planning for an event as much as they enjoy the actual event. And, they tend to start things early and love 'getting it done'.

That need for closure may even drive them to accomplishments.

People who prefer **Perceiving** seek to experience the world, not organize it. They look at the world and see options that need to be explored. These folks tend to explore possibilities and may not want to finish something because there may be another option they haven't found yet. They may be deadline-driven and really get an adrenaline rush at the deadline. These folks fight against starting early because they do their best work at the end – faster and better.

Remember, we all use both attitudes, but usually not with equal comfort.

Recognizing your most natural traits, really starting to understand those traits, embracing the truth of who you are, and recognizing that others are different is a very special place to be. It opens the door for you to be the best version of yourself!

AHA MOMENT

I used to really beat myself up for being a procrastinator. I have the intention to work early and meet deadlines ahead of time, but the reality is that I'm always working furiously at the deadline. I have an adrenaline rush, and I move quicker and with more effectiveness. When I became certified to coach the Myers-Briggs® personality index, I realized that I naturally work best under pressure. Then, I:

1. quit feeling guilt about procrastinating, and
2. built time in my calendar to accommodate that natural instinct to work close to the deadline.

I realize now that I honestly work faster and produce better results when I am at the deadline. "Procrastination" is no longer in my vocabulary. Instead of guilt and self-ridicule, I embrace that as my truth and work in the way I'm at my best.

✅ LET'S DO IT!
ACTIVITY

There are many types of personality assessments online. There are links at my website to my favorite assessments:

www.expandwithpurpose.com/
discovering-your-purpose

Whenever you take any self-assessment, answer the questions quickly and instinctively. Remember the results are simply an output of your answers. So read the outcome with an open mind. Consider what you agree with and what 'jumps out at you'. If you disagree with something, that's ok — but I recommend that you first be very self-aware. Do you disagree because you deny the truth or really see yourself differently?

Make notes about recurring words, phrases, or themes. What feels true for you? What answers questions for you?

Recurring words, phrases, or themes

What feels true for you?

_____

_____

_____

_____

_____

_____

What answers questions for you?

_____

_____

_____

_____

_____

_____

Identifying the Values that Motivate You Within

V alues are internal motivators—they explain your choices and behaviors. We see behaviors, hear words, and see outcomes of decisions, but those are all external results of our internal motivators. We can't see our values, but they do exist. We hold them dear to our heart, and they are behind the decisions and choices we make.

They are personal; they exist from our beliefs, our worldview, our experiences, the culture we were raised in, and the values of our parents or mentors. Values change over time; as our experiences change and as we grow, our values change. Do you value the same things you valued one, ten, twenty years ago? Of course not; your experiences and influences change you as you grow.

It's important to recognize your values because when you do, you understand more about why you do the things you do. For example, if family is a core value, you may make decisions with your spouse/partner or children in mind, not only yourself. If, however, achievement is a higher priority core value, then you may make different career decisions.

When we are conscious of our personal core values, we use them intentionally to measure alternatives against them. For example, if family is a core value for you, and you are conscious of it, you may choose (or not choose) a job opportunity based on the impact it will have on your family. If you aren't conscious of how important this value is to you, you may find yourself in a job that does not align with that core value of family. And, thus, you may find yourself disappointed, frustrated or just on edge.

If you find yourself at odds with something in your life, examining your underlying feelings will often lead you to discovering a misalignment with your values.

Your emotional triggers often come from someone not respecting your values. If someone says they will do something then drops the ball, I have an emotional and immediate reaction. I now realize this directly relates back to my personal value of accountability. Knowing that connection allows me to manage the intensity

AHA MOMENT

I was leading a marketing team who was able to outline my values in respect to understanding what I expected as a team lead. They had a list I later referred to as my "rules of the road" for this team. When I looked at the list they created, I was in awe of how profoundly it aligned with my inner values. For example, having, knowing, and meeting deadlines was one of the attributes my team shared with new members, and it was important to me. It directly aligned to my personal value of accountability. That value has shown up in more places than only my expectations of my team. It shows up with my students when they are late with assignments—and when they go the extra mile. My energy toward them changes and I feel different motivating emotions that are situational, but they all tie back to this value of accountability.

of my emotional response. If someone drops the ball, it doesn't necessarily mean it's a personal attack against me and my need for accountability. By bringing the value, the trigger, and the response to my consciousness, I can better respond and interact more positively with others.

I can also communicate the importance of that value to those around me. In my classroom, that relates to late work. I have a strong reaction to students missing deadlines and then later wanting to make up the work, or get extra credit. So now, I clearly communicate my "no late work" policy and *why*—I expect them to be as accountable to their work as I am to their education. It's a shared responsibility. The up-front communication helps us be on the same page from the beginning. Before I realized the connection, I allowed for late work and then was constantly frustrated by accepting it. That reaction was exasperating to me and unfair to students.

Now it's your turn! On the next few pages, you will see many common values and definitions. View the list and consider the top five values that motivate you. These represent the main reasons you do what you do. You can also take a Values Quiz at my website:

www.expandwithpurpose.com/
discovering-your-purpose

Values

Accountability

Being obliged to answer for one's own actions

Achievement

A sense of accomplishment, mastery, goal achievement

Activity

Fast-paced, highly active work

Advancement

Growth and promotion resulting from work well done

Adventure

New and challenging opportunities, excitement, risk

Aesthetics

Appreciation of beauty in things, ideas, surroundings, personal space

Affiliation

Interaction with people, recognition as a member of a particular group, involvement, belonging

Affluence

High income, financial success, prosperity

Authority

Position and power to control events and other people's activities

Autonomy	Ability to act independently with few constraints, self-sufficiency, self-reliance, ability to make most decisions and choices
Balance	Lifestyle that allows for a balance of time for self, family, work, and community
Beauty	An appreciation for and seeing the beauty in all things
Challenge	Continually facing complex and demanding tasks and problems
Change & Variation	Absence of routine; work responsibilities, daily activities, or settings that change frequently; unpredictability
Collaboration	Close, cooperative working relationships with groups
Community	Serving and supporting a purpose that supersedes personal desires, "making a difference"

Competency	Demonstrating high proficiency and knowledge, showing above-average effectiveness and efficiency at tasks
Competition	Rivalry with winning as the goal
Compassion	Understanding the suffering of others and wanting to do something about it
Cooperation	Working together for a common purpose
Courage	Willingness to stand up for one's beliefs
Creativity	A high degree of innovation, imagination, and originality; discovering, developing, or designing new ideas, formats, programs, or things
Dedication	The act of binding yourself (intellectually or emotionally) to a course of action
Diverse Perspectives	Unusual ideas and opinions, points of view that may not seem right or be popular at first but bear fruit in the long run
Duty	Respect for authority, rules, and regulations

Economic Security	Steady and secure employment, adequate financial reward, low risk experiences
Empathy	Feeling concern for and understanding another's situation or feelings
Enjoyment	Fun, joy, and laughter
Faith	A strong belief in a supernatural power or powers that control human destiny
Fame	Prominence, being well known
Family	Spending time with partner, children, parents, or extended family
Freedom	The power to act, speak, or think without externally imposed restraints
Friendship	Close personal relationships with others
Happiness	Well-being and contentment; pleasurable
Health	Physical and mental well-being, vitality
Helpfulness	Sense of concern, support, and outreach to the needs of others; helping people attain their goals

Honesty	A high regard for fairness, straight-forwardness, sincerity, truthfulness
Humor	The ability to laugh at oneself and find humor in all things
Independence	Freedom from control or influence of another or others, self-sufficient
Influence	Having an impact or effect on the attitudes or opinions of other people, persuasiveness
Inner Harmony	Happiness, contentment, being at peace with oneself
Integrity	The quality or state of being of sound moral principle; acting in accordance with moral and ethical standards; uprightness, honesty, sincerity, truth; trustworthiness
Justice	Fairness, balance, equality, "doing the right thing"
Knowledge	Seeking and learning new information and insights; the pursuit of understanding, skill, and expertise; continuous learning

Life	An appreciation and respect for all living things
Love	Strong personal feelings of caring and affection; intimacy
Loyalty	Faithfulness to another person or group; dedication to individuals, traditions, or organizations
Morality	Desire for high ethical standards; a strong sense of right and wrong
Order	Stability, routine, predictability, clear lines of authority, standardized procedures
Patience	The capacity for enduring hardship or inconvenience
Personal Development	Dedication to maximizing one's potential
Physical Fitness	Staying in shape through exercise and physical activity
Power	Ability to lead, direct, persuade, control
Professionalism	Commitment to quality; pride in your work

Recognition	To receive special attention, respect, and admiration; to feel important; to receive positive feedback and public credit for work well done
Religion	Belonging to an organized religion
Respect	Unbiased consideration and regard for the rights, values, beliefs, and property of all people
Responsibility	Being answerable to someone for something or being responsible for one's own conduct; dependability; reliability; accountability for results
Security	Having the essentials you need to live and be safe
Self-Respect	Pride, self-esteem, sense of personal identity
Service	Useful labor that does not produce a tangible commodity; to help others for no personal gain
Spirituality	A way of living that emphasizes a constant awareness of the spiritual dimension of nature; moral fulfillment

Status Being respected for one's job or one's association with a prestigious group or organization

Success Attainment of professional position, favor, or eminence; achieving your goals

Trustworthiness Dependability, deserving of confidence

Wealth Desire for substantial monetary income

Wisdom The ability to apply knowledge, experience, understanding, common sense, and insight

Work Deriving great value from your job

This list revised from I Care Values. n.d. "Values Activity Card Set." Accessed 2009. http://www.icarevalues.org/Value%20Cards%20v4.d.pdf

✓ LET'S DO IT!
ACTIVITY

Now it's your turn. View the values above, paying attention to your personal meaning of the word, not necessarily the given definition. The definitions are here for guidance, but you may interpret the words differently. You may also recognize a value not listed here; make this your own.

List five values that resonate with you the most:

① _____

② _____

③ _____

④ _____

⑤ _____

NEXT STEP: DIGGING DEEPER

1

VALUE:

RELEVANCE:

Our values change over time, as we are exposed to new situations. Our backgrounds contribute to our values. Why is this value important to you?

_____

_____

_____

DEMONSTRATION:

How do you see this value demonstrated in your work or personal life (current or past)?

_____

_____

_____

TRIGGERS:

When others do not honor our core values, we tend to have an emotional response that might show up in various ways. Describe what happens when someone does not honor this value.

_____

_____

_____

_____

_____

_____

_____

_____

2

VALUE:

RELEVANCE:

Our values change over time, as we are exposed to new situations. Our backgrounds contribute to our values. Why is this value important to you?

_____

_____

_____

DEMONSTRATION:

How do you see this value demonstrated in your work or personal life (current or past)?

_____

_____

_____

TRIGGERS:

When others do not honor our core values, we tend to have an emotional response that might show up in various ways. Describe what happens when someone does not honor this value.

_____

_____

_____

_____

_____

_____

_____

_____

_____

3   VALUE:

RELEVANCE:

Our values change over time, as we are exposed to new situations. Our backgrounds contribute to our values. Why is this value important to you?

_____

_____

_____

DEMONSTRATION:

How do you see this value demonstrated in your work or personal life (current or past)?

_____

_____

_____

TRIGGERS:

When others do not honor our core values, we tend to have an emotional response that might show up in various ways. Describe what happens when someone does not honor this value.

_____

_____

_____

_____

_____

_____

_____

_____

4

VALUE:

RELEVANCE:

Our values change over time, as we are exposed to new situations. Our backgrounds contribute to our values. Why is this value important to you?

_____

_____

_____

DEMONSTRATION:

How do you see this value demonstrated in your work or personal life (current or past)?

_____

_____

_____

TRIGGERS:

When others do not honor our core values, we tend to have an emotional response that might show up in various ways. Describe what happens when someone does not honor this value.

_____

_____

_____

_____

_____

_____

_____

_____

5 VALUE:

RELEVANCE:

Our values change over time, as we are exposed to new situations. Our backgrounds contribute to our values. Why is this value important to you?

_____

_____

_____

DEMONSTRATION:

How do you see this value demonstrated in your work or personal life (current or past)?

_____

_____

_____

TRIGGERS:

When others do not honor our core values, we tend to have an emotional response that might show up in various ways. Describe what happens when someone does not honor this value.

_____

_____

_____

_____

_____

_____

_____

Now that you recognize the values, the triggers, and your responses, look for where they show up in your life. Remember them and use them consciously to guide your decisions.

TRIGGERS:

When others do not honor our core values, we tend to have an emotional response that might show up in various ways. Describe what happens when someone does not honor this value.

_____

_____

_____

_____

_____

_____

_____

Now that you recognize the values, the triggers, and your responses, look for where they show up in your life. Remember them and use them consciously to guide your decisions.

Owning Your Unique Strengths

Each of us possess strengths and skills that are natural to us. We have all experienced activities where we are "in the zone" and realize accomplishment while really enjoying what we are doing. These are the areas of our unique strengths—those things we do with ease, we do them well, and we love doing them.

When people understand their strengths, they can better apply them in all areas of their lives. This application of strengths provides value to oneself as well as to those around you. When we are working within our strengths, we work faster, we produce better results, we make more impact, and we work with an energy that creates innovation and success.

Think of those times when you know you are working in areas that are not your strengths. We work slower, it's harder, it takes more mental energy, it creates fatigue, and stress ensues. It can take longer to create the results we want.

While each of us have unique strengths, the reality is that many of us don't recognize them for the real strengths they are. We don't appreciate our abilities as strengths. I think we are taught that success comes with hard work and this ideal that we must work hard is instilled in us as children. As children, we are taught to improve our weaknesses instead of increasing our strengths.

I encourage you to focus now on those strengths and skills that are natural for you. Sometimes people can immediately tell me what those are, and other times people really struggle to identify what they are great at doing. There seems to be this awkwardness in admitting what we are great at doing. Why do you think that is? Maybe it feels arrogant or self-promoting. The idea of finding your passion, managing to your strengths, and positive psychology are intertwined theories. These practices have been around a long time in the areas of psychology, education, career development, and the field of organizational development.

AHA MOMENT

I was working on a project team, and we were focused on this idea of applying our unique strengths to our work. One day two of us, sitting next to each other, realized that we both had this pile of work that was frustrating us. My responsibility was to reconcile the balance of our postal account daily, as the statements arrived. These statements were piling up in a drawer, and I was avoiding doing it until it was essential. My partner was taking customer service-type calls and every time the phone rang, he wanted to do anything he could to avoid them.

I remember the day we looked at each other and agreed to trade these two tasks. He eagerly balanced those statements daily as they arrived. I took those customer service calls with pleasure, problem solving for customers daily. We worked well together for years, we constantly traded jobs to attempt to stay in alignment with our strengths. The work got done faster and better, and we were energized and no longer avoiding our tasks and feeling guilty.

A Brief Early History of Strengths Approaches

There are many resources for identifying your unique strengths. Beginning in 1911, Bernard Haldane initiated research in strengths and positive psychology research, and he became legendary in career development circles.

Positive psychology is a field started in the 1940s with focus on youth in schools, and for decades, we have seen the rise of strengths-based ways of working in organizations.

Research on strengths theory has existed explicitly in the management literature for more than sixty years. In 1947, Haldane wrote an article in the *Harvard Business Review* that expressed his belief that the core reason for lack of engagement at work was that management and leadership did not understand how to identify and apply employees' strengths in ways that met the individual's needs.

In 1967, twenty years after Haldane, Peter Drucker wrote that "the unique purpose of organization is to make strength productive" (Drucker, 1967, 60). Drucker contended that by identifying and combining the strengths of different individuals in a way that made their weaknesses irrelevant, the organization was stronger.

Decades ago, I was introduced to Dan Sullivan, founder of Strategic Coach. He describes Unique Abilities® as having four characteristics:

- A superior ability that other people notice and value
- Love doing it and want to do it as much as possible
- Energizing for you and others around you
- You keep getting better, never running out of possibilities for further improvement

How to Identify Your Strengths

I encourage you to think about your work, courses, volunteer work, and home life. Think about those things you love to do and do it "in the zone." Think about things you've done that make time fly by. These are your unique strengths – your natural talents.

As well, there are things we do that drain our energy and leave us depleted. Right now, as you think about the things you need to do, what energizes you and what feels like an energy drain? Remember the Braggart, the Humble, and the Confident (Chapter 2)? The Braggart looks at themself and sees all things as strengths. The Humble looks at themselves and sees most things as weaknesses. The Confident looks at themselves and sees honesty and reality – both their strengths and their weaknesses. They don't apologize for them, they just recognize their truth.

That is my hope for you; that you recognize your truth in this exercise.

✅ LET'S DO IT! ACTIVITY

Consider your strengths: those things you love to do, people ask you to do them, time flies, and you would do them without being paid to do them:

A1 _____

A2 _____

A3 _____

A4 _____

A5 _____

Next, consider those things you really aren't great at doing, things you dread being asked to do, things you don't want to do and that your mental energy feels drained when you think about doing them:

B1 _____

B2 _____

B3 _____

B4 _____

B5 _____

How can you stop doing these things? To stop doing things we aren't great at, we have options:

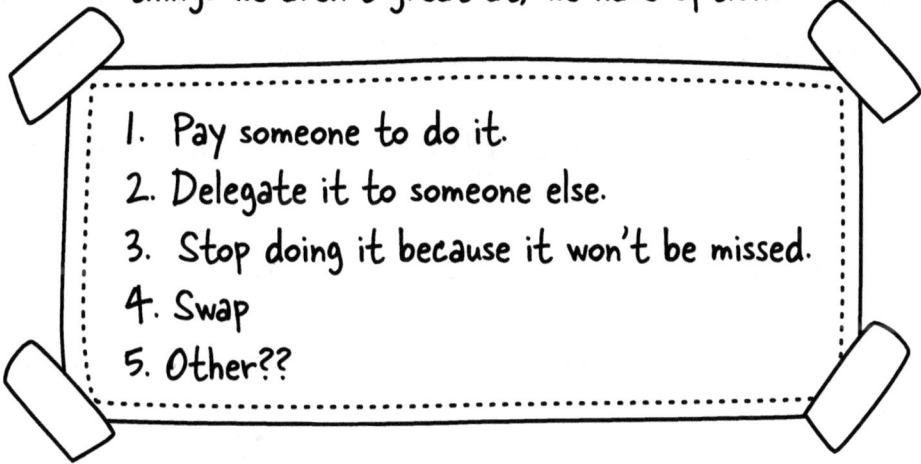

1. Pay someone to do it.
2. Delegate it to someone else.
3. Stop doing it because it won't be missed.
4. Swap
5. Other??

For each of the items in Section B, identify a solution to stop doing it. Maybe you can't stop doing it today, but set a time line and start working on a plan to remove it from your time and effort.

(**Example:** I will pay my son to mow the grass by the end of May.)

STRATEGY: **DEADLINE:**

B1 I will _____ by _____

B2 I will _____ by _____

B3 I will _____ by _____

B4 I will _____ by _____

B5 I will _____ by _____

Where can you find more ways to do the things you love? For Section A, identify at least one place in your life, now or in the future, where you can do more of those things:

STRATEGY: **DEADLINE:**

(**A1**) I will _____ by _____

(**A2**) I will _____ by _____

(**A3**) I will _____ by _____

(**A4**) I will _____ by _____

(**A5**) I will _____ by _____

Chapter 9

Finding Your Passions

What are you passionate about? What do you love to do? Passions mean something different to different people. I think that passion is summed up in the things I'm interested in—the things I would do even if I didn't get paid (and could afford to do that!). I think we confuse passion with our jobs sometimes. I may be passionate about something that doesn't connect to my job. We confuse the skills we have with passion. I'm really good at developing systems, but I wouldn't say I'm passionate about it!

Back when you were a child, what did you dream about doing? Before life got in the way, how did you think about spending your time? What do you search online about, what books are on your bookshelf? We tend to gravitate toward the things that we are passionate about—even if we don't do it on purpose! To consider your passions, first put aside, just for a minute, all the responsibilities you have, the expectations of the people in your life, your own expectations of yourself, and the reasons you must continue doing what you are doing. Put aside the fact that you have to pay the mortgage and make the car payment. Whatever is holding you to your need for keeping the status quo going, just set it aside for a few minutes and play. Let's explore what you would do if you could spend your days doing anything you found enjoyment in.

My extraverted friend seems full of energy and passion in everything she considers. I, on the other hand, in my introverted, cerebral self, used to think I wasn't passionate because I didn't feel physical excited energy on any topics. But I learned that passion isn't necessarily about external energy. I think it's a fire in the belly. I'm passionate about helping people see their potential but I don't yell it from the rooftops. That's not my personability or my style. It shows up in one on one conversations though...all the time. I realized that 'passion' is personal and how it shows up in our lives is personal and unique.

✓ LET'S DO IT!
ACTIVITY

Complete each of the statements—don't think too hard. Don't worry about how it sounds, just go with your first instinct. Give yourself permission to be real, no matter what anyone else might think or how crazy (or boring) it sounds to you!

When I was a kid, I dreamed of...

I love books and movies about...

If I stayed home from work for a week, I'd...

Most people don't know this about me,
but I really enjoy...

I'll

My friends or family call me when they need help with...

I can teach someone to...

If I were to make a homemade gift,
it would involve...

I haven't done this frequently, but I really enjoy...

The closest I come to a runner's high is when I'm...

If I won first prize in a talent show, it would be for...

List that choice below as #1 and repeat the process
to identify your top five passions:

1. _____
2. _____
3. _____
4. _____
5. _____

Revised from Attwood, J., and C. Attwood. 2008

Consider these five passions. Is there anything here that connects to your recent or past thoughts? Does it bring any other passions to mind?

_____

_____

_____

_____

_____

_____

_____

_____

_____

_____

Chapter 10

Discovering Your Purpose

The path to living in your purpose begins with really knowing yourself. It begins with our very real, bared open, assessment of self:

Skill + Motivators + Personality + Passions = Purpose

Pulling it all together and being able to articulate our purpose is the next step.

Framing your purpose into a statement enables you to claim it, know it, remember it, and keep it in the front of your mind so you can use it to measure your opportunities against it. Summarize the four areas of purpose into one place, merge them together, and identify your purpose.

Tammy

Personality

- I get energy introvertedly from Self & Thoughts
- I take In Information Concretely Seeing & Knowing It. Need to know WHY
- Decisions balance on right/wrong, logical path, and impact on others
- I see processes and paths in front of me as a process of creating systems and routines. Deadline driven

Passions

- Learning, Teaching, Helping Others Grow

Strengths

- Teaching, Organizing, Processes/Systems/People Fit and Motivating for Efficiency

Values

- Faith, Family, Fun, Accountability, Growth

MY PURPOSE IS:

To help others see the potential in themselves or their business and help them develop a path to be more tomorrow than they were yesterday, to fulfill their purpose in the world.

I apply my purpose today in these areas:

Teaching

- Help others to see their own potential and ability for learning and success to find their place in the world and be comfortable in their own voice.

Consulting

- Help entrepreneurs to see the mission and economic value of their idea in the marketplace; to see a path to personal and business alignment.
- Provide in-depth Leadership Development Programs for mission focused organizations to encourage leaders at all levels to see incremental and immediate change with alignment in values and organizational objectives.

✅ LET'S DO IT! ACTIVITY

Now it's your turn. Complete the following table, first with a summary of the four previous areas, then by pulling it together into your purpose as defined today. Next, identify where you use your purpose today and where you might look to use it in the future.

(1) For each of the 4 areas, go back to your previous activities and write themes, key words, phrases.

Personality

_____

_____

_____

_____

Passions

_____

_____

Strengths

_____

_____

_____

Values

_____

_____

_____

② As you consider these 4 areas, look for common themes, repeated ideas. Let your mind take it all in, observe it, consider experiences where these show up. Then work to create a statement taking these ideas into your unique purpose.

My purpose is to [what] because [why].
What=what you do naturally
Why =the motivations that drive you

MY PURPOSE IS TO:

_____

_____

_____

_____

I apply my purpose today in these areas:

_____

_____

_____

Places or ways I can apply my purpose in the future:

_____

_____

_____

_____

Remember those limiting beliefs you wrote down and put away in Chapter 1? Pull them back out and reconsider them, one by one. Are any invalid now? Can you reframe them into liberating truths? Can you change your view of reality?

When I started my journey toward working 90 percent of my time within my unique purpose, I had to maintain a fairly significant income (my limiting belief) for my family to maintain the way of life we created. However, there were some places we could cut back. I created three income budgets based on our living expenses: Worst Case (e.g., the least money I could make and we'd survive), Best Case (more money than I was currently making), and Optimal Case (somewhere in between). Those three scenarios helped me work within a span of expectation instead of solely focusing on one income level. When I backed into it, keeping my purpose first, I figured out I could do a few different things to make up the income I needed. Previously, I had a single narrow mindset: I had to get another job doing the same things for someone else. Instead, I started on a journey of experimenting, trying new things. This ultimately led me to teaching and coaching full time.

I think people sometimes put up limitations before they ever give themselves a real chance at creatively reaching for their dreams.

Memorize your purpose! Write it down. Carry it with you. Be creative in a way that suits you – write it out and put it in your wallet. Design a 'business card' for your purpose, create a poster in Canva, paint it, draw it...

Try it out on people. Hold your head high and say it: "My purpose is to help people be better today than they were yesterday and guide them to understanding their own unique purpose, personally and in their businesses."

Refine it—consider it a "living document" that may change over time. That means that you tweak it until you feel comfortable saying it and striving toward living in that space. If you feel vulnerable, process that. Why? What's going on inside that is behind the vulnerability or the emotion?

11

Finding Your Voice

Finding my voice and feeling really confident in it was one of the more powerful milestones in my life. I used to spend time and energy trying to emulate mentors or measure up to those I respected. I worried about how motivating I was, if I was "enough" for the job. I was my biggest critic, and I compared myself to those I looked up to. Until one day, when I realized that I was enough. I have my own style, my own voice, and my own way of looking at the world. And there are people who respond positively to me and my voice.

Your voice represents your authentic self. Own it, recognize how it works for you, and trust yourself.

AHA MOMENT

I was planning a team retreat and had the agenda and accommodations in place. I carefully worked through the objectives, the food to accommodate everyone, and inserted fun throughout the three-day offsite retreat. As I thought about how to introduce the retreat and get everyone started with the right message, I felt real shortcomings as to my ability to motivate and inspire the team. In that space of insecurity, I asked my boss to speak for a few minutes, encouraging and inspiring the team as we left the office for the working retreat. While I felt confident in my leadership, I didn't feel confident in my motivating and inspiring "send-off." He could be extremely motivating and had a talent for energizing people.

As I sat listening to him share his own version of our "send-off," my wide, excited eyes grew wider as if watching a train wreck happening before me. His agenda didn't resemble my intent at all, and I would spend the next three days convincing people as to the real purpose of our team's objectives and reassuring them of their value.

I remember walking out of the conference room, through the big glass front doors to my car, thinking very clearly, "On my worst day, I could have done better than that!" In that moment, I realized that MY voice worked for me, and I didn't need anyone else's style to accomplish what I was there for. It was a life-changing moment of clarity and confidence. My style is not an accident.

12

OK...Now What??

You should measure yourself through the lens of your purpose. Surround yourself with people who believe in the power of you. Who support and connect to you. Knowledge comes from others, mentors, your faith, and your own instinct. Call it what you will: Holy Spirit, instinct, the universe, your higher power, your belief system. If we are in a place of higher consciousness to listen quietly, spirit and soul guides us. Watch for the patterns, the signs. Hearing the same message over and over? Pay attention and breathe through it, embracing the message in its entirety and not through the lens of skepticism or self-doubt.

American author, spiritual leader, and political activist, Marianne Williamson wrote: "Our deepest fear is not that we are inadequate. Our deepest fear is that we are powerful beyond measure. It is our light, not our darkness that most frightens us. We ask ourselves, 'Who am I to be brilliant, gorgeous, talented and fabulous?' Actually, who are you not to be? You are a child of God. Your playing small doesn't serve the world. And as we let our own light shine, we unconsciously give other people permission to do the same. As we are liberated from our own fear, our presence automatically liberates others." (Williamson, 1996)

So then, to live in your light, and your greatness, where is the balance between boastfulness and truth? Humble confidence is present in the knowing our truth while respectfully knowing the truth of those around us.

Be the author of your own story. In his Stanford commencement speech, Steve Jobs (2005), said, "Don't waste time living someone else's dream."

Identifying your purpose leads you to your dream. One Christmas, my daughter asked for several books by Jon Gordon. One little red book caught my attention as I was wrapping her gifts, so I paused to read it. In his book, *One Word That Will Change Your Life*, Gordon (2013), discusses how focusing on one word for the year will give you purpose and intentionality. Instead of setting resolutions or goals, he says, meditatively and with intention, identify one word, or theme, and live in that focus for the year. Fairly quickly, the word **TODAY** popped into my mind. The irony of the word is that I'm a planner, a controller, and one that strives for future goals. At the time, we were on a very defined path of selling our home and moving out of state, to the family's homesteaded farm. This was to significantly change the course of our lives. But, willing to give this idea of considering a theme for the year a chance, I wrote the word **TODAY** in big black letters on an index card and posted it above my desk.

At the same time, I was trying, with little movement from my dissertation chair, to finish a PhD, and I had filed a formal complaint with the school to change chairs. As an educator, that's a very hard thing to do, and it was taking a long time. At this point, I had given the entire degree over to God, and had truly been willing to stop wasting my energy getting nowhere if it was not what I should finish. Giving it to God, I vowed to let it go if my ego was in the way and I needed to do something else. (Achievement is a core value for me, so you can imagine how painful and hard this was.) I tried to focus on **TODAY** instead of tomorrow's plan, and we put our house on the market in mid-March. Life continued down the path we had set until a four o'clock phone call in late April, announcing my new chair, easing my fears and frustrations, with assurances of movement and doctoral completion. I was on cloud nine! Until eight o'clock the next morning, when a doctor pulled his stool up close and explained that my husband's aggressive, rare cancer would need immediate surgery and treatment. Soon, we were told that the next twelve months would be very focused on his treatment and care, and everything in our lives would center around that care. In a whirlwind of doctor appointments and tests, life got reorganized fast—and all I could do was focus on **TODAY** because, in very real reality, I couldn't do anything more than get through each day an hour at a time.

Broken, on my knees, I questioned God's timing for the first time in my life. Our house was on the market, my PhD just got energy behind it, we would be consumed with healing and recovery, and I would be balancing work with caretaking as well as growing a start-up company.

God reminded me of Matthew 6:25-34

Therefore do not worry about tomorrow, for tomorrow will worry about itself.

☀AHA MOMENT

I realized the key was balance: if we have no vision, we wander. But, if we only look at tomorrow, we miss today. We can spend so much time focused on the dream, and even the path to get there, that we can lose the moment of today. Sometimes, all we can do is get through today. There are also times to focus on tomorrow. Balance and awareness...

In the midst of that chaotic year, standing in the grocery line, I remember thinking, "Why have I found myself standing here, behind a frazzled mother and fit-throwing two-year-old?" It was a great reminder of how, too often, we look inward instead of being present in the moment. When I'm focused on my own issues, my own path, I miss the opportunity that may be in front of me. For I've been the frazzled mother of a fit-throwing two-year-old in the cashier line before. Oh, how an empathetic and helpful person could have impacted this young, embarrassed mother more positively than the harried cashier and the eye-rolling, head-shaking professional behind me. With a smile, I said something to the effect of, "We've all been there. While it gets better, you've still got fit-throwing teens to look forward to." Brevity broke the tension and embarrassment for that young mother. Be present in the moment. Be to others what they need.

We can so easily overlook the opportunity to make a difference today—the cashier who needs a friendly face, to know how glad you are that they're there. For if I choose the cashier over the self-checkout, there is a reason, and the reason is important although I may not recognize it if I'm not living in the moment.

There is power in balancing *today* with the vision of tomorrow. I believe in both, for if we don't know where we're going, we drift and cross our fingers that we end up there safely. Oh my goodness! How scary to think about that; even as I write it, my heart skips a beat. And yet, I also know this pressure, self-incrimination, and overwhelming feeling of tunnel vision to stick with the plan—or the path I've deemed appropriate. Maybe the vision of the dream is less clear. It's more of looking at the future through a driving rain storm, only seeing ten feet in front of you at a time. Then the next ten feet, and the next. It's like eyeglasses covered in humidity, as they are less sharp, my vision is blurrier, and I have to use all my senses instead of relying only on my eyes. My instincts kick in. I'm more aware of the moment and what's immediately around me.

Being a passenger on a motorcycle is also a lot like balancing the destination and being in the moment. As a passenger in a car, there is less awareness of where we're going, where we're at, and more awareness of what's going on inside the car: the radio station, the GPS, voices, passengers reading, movies playing, phones glowing. When you are on a motorcycle, there is nothing to do but *be* in the moment. Your senses are heightened, and all you can do is look around you. As the passenger, you can't see ahead as well as the driver, so you smell everything more keenly (including the road kill), you notice the people you pass, you get lost in the nature as it flies by. When I hear the jingle of motorcycle keys, I run to make sure I get "in" on the ride, for it's one of the most sensory moments, reminding me to just be in the moment.

For life is really only a collection of moments and relationships. The stuff we do during our day either creates positive momentum in those moments, it stalls us, or it inhibits our movement. Likewise, our interactions with others enhances our self or the other person, provides neutrality, or inhibits our or others' growth. Neutrality is interesting, for sometimes we need that nothingness for regeneration. We need the pause to laugh, to sit quietly together, or to dance as though no one is watching.

In all, remember to stay in your unique purpose as much as you can.

"Don't waste time living someone else's dream."
—Steve Jobs

"When people forget their why, they lose their way."
—Michael Hyatt

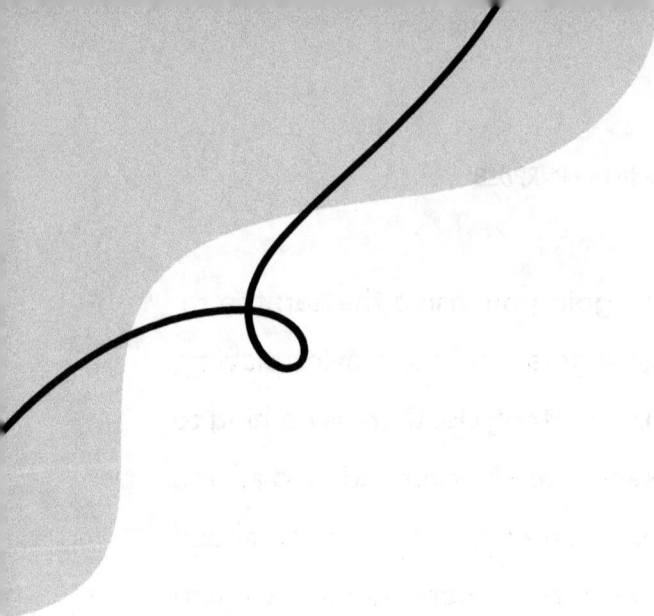

References

Attwood, J., and C. Attwood. 2008. *The Passion Test: The Effort-less Path to Discovering Your Life Purpose.*

Drucker, P. F. 1967. *The Effective Executive.* London: Heinemann.

Gordon, J. 2013. *One Word that Will Change Your Life.*

I Care Values. n.d. "Values Activity Card Set." Accessed 2009. http://www.icarevalues.org/Value%20Cards%20v4.d.pdf

Jobs, S. 2005. "Stanford Commencement Address"

McCaulley, M. H. 2000. "Myers-Briggs Type Indicator: A Bridge Between Counseling and Consulting." *Consulting Psychology Journal: Practice and Research* 52(2): 117–132. https://doi.org/10.1037/1061-4087.52.2.117.

Sullivan, C. 1995. *Focusing Your Unique Ability.* Strategic Coach.

Williamson, Marianne. 1996. *A Return to Love.* New York: Harper Collins.

Notes

About the Author

TAMMY OGREN is a Life Coach, College Professor, and a Management Consultant.

In sharing her own experiences, struggles, and successes, she helps people discover their personal meaning in the context of divine purpose. In her unique way, she has spent nearly 4 decades helping people see their uniqueness and using practical, actionable steps to applying their purpose with intention and meaning to change their lives, their career, their businesses, and their volunteer lives. In her work with students, educators, professionals, employees, business owners, leaders, and retirees has demonstrated the success of her 5 step program to developing a tomorrow that is better than their yesterday. Contact Tammy on Instagram @ExpandWithPurpose or online at ExpandWithPurpose.com.

Discover your Purpose with Personal Coaching.

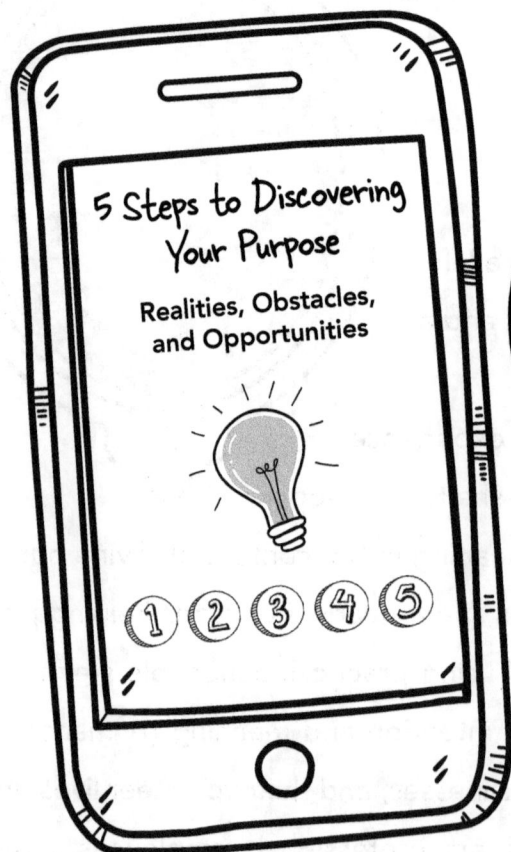

5 Steps to Discovering
Your Purpose

**Realities, Obstacles,
and Opportunities**

(1) (2) (3) (4) (5)

Featuring
Tammy Ogren

Check out Tammy's individualized programs at:

www.expandwithpurpose.com/
discovering-your-purpose

Discover your Purpose with Personal Coaching.

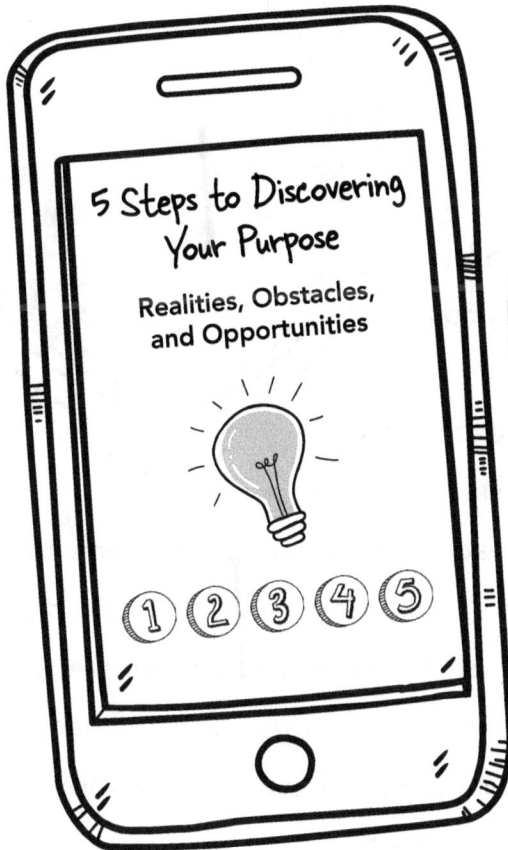

5 Steps to Discovering
Your Purpose

Realities, Obstacles,
and Opportunities

1 2 3 4 5

Featuring
Tammy Ogren

Check out Tammy's individualized programs at:

www.expandwithpurpose.com/
discovering-your-purpose

About the Author

TAMMY OGREN is a Life Coach, College Professor, and a Management Consultant.

In sharing her own experiences, struggles, and successes, she helps people discover their personal meaning in the context of divine purpose. In her unique way, she has spent nearly 4 decades helping people see their uniqueness and using practical, actionable steps to applying their purpose with intention and meaning to change their lives, their career, their businesses, and their volunteer lives. In her work with students, educators, professionals, employees, business owners, leaders, and retirees has demonstrated the success of her 5 step program to developing a tomorrow that is better than their yesterday. Contact Tammy on Instagram @ExpandWithPurpose or online at ExpandWithPurpose.com.

www.ingramcontent.com/pod-product-compliance
Lightning Source LLC
LaVergne TN
LVHW081327060426
835513LV00012B/1222

*9 7 9 8 9 8 7 9 8 0 8 0 4 *